In Us We Tru

CU01432762

Copyright Melissa

ISBN: 978-1-7384786-0-6 (Paperback)

First edition published in the UK by Melissa Grewar The Spiritual Engineer 2024

Content by Melissa Grewar The Spiritual Engineer
Images by Melissa Grewar The Spiritual Engineer and
Ann English & Create Intrigue
Published by Melissa Grewar The Spiritual Engineer

For Einstein (aka John)
If it wasn't for you,
I couldn't have written this book.
On behalf of everyone and everything,
we thank you.

From Melissa's earliest memories, a spiritual connection guided her thoughts. She wanted to understand life better, so she studied different religions. She became most interested in spiritualism.

In her career, she discovered her true strength: helping people overcome societal limitations. She used spiritual practices to help others with their mental and emotional well-being. She also helped them with their trust issues.

The onset of the Covid pandemic marked a turning point. Melissa embraced the gift of time and learned spiritual skills through online workshops. Her purpose in life was to help people by healing and offering spiritual guidance. This led to writing "In Us We Trust" where she can reach a wider audience.

Melissa

The Unity Symbol

The Unity Symbol consists of 7 elements. Together, they represent the meaning of life and our existence within the Universe. To understand your purpose and place in the Universe, it's important to know why they matter.

The triangle represents balance and stability by combining body, mind, and spirit. It can also symbolise the Father, Son, and Holy Spirit in other diverse contexts. Other representations include fire, air, and water through the forces of nature. The powerful simplicity of the triangle is the balance of female and male energies. The triangle suggests a change so all may transform. From the early stages of the earth's initiation, you ascend to intuitive enlightenment. You achieve this by changing your perspective.

The square also holds diverse meanings. All four sides are equal and create order, making the shape balanced and stable. This shape has provided a traditional and sound foundation for generations. The square also represents fire, air, water and earth. In sacred geometry, it represents cosmic order and perfection. The square inside the triangle is essential. It shows how we currently see and understand the world around us. The way we limit our needs is what sets our desires apart.

The circle is a powerful symbol that resonates more with intuitive principles. It represents wholeness, perpetual and timeless energies in a never-ending cycle. Individuals see it as a sacred symbol representing the Universe or finding oneself. It can also mean fostering inclusivity or protection by creating healthy boundaries. This symbol can also represent the chaos that affects how we live. To understand ourselves, we must go within. To understand, we must break down all elements of ourselves. Analysing the deconstruction of what no longer works creates clarity, understanding and progress.

The Infinity symbol is a desire for peace through harmonious actions. It fosters a sense of unity and understanding among diverse communities. When we choose nonviolent reconciliation, it shows our commitment to solving problems. It evokes a sense of hope and optimism with a vision for a better future. Everyone and everything is equal in different ways because we all have a purpose. Harmony happens when everything in the Universe works together. Planets, energy, people, animals, and plants all work together to help each other evolve.

The dividing line separates these physical spaces. In our world, they represent personal limits. The line also represents conflicts or divisions in our communities. With clarity and order, we can offer everything structure through organisation. This format helps decision-making from ideological and theoretical opinions. It serves as a point of choice from legal and ethical limits. This dividing line can protect one side from threats, like a barrier or boundary. It can show change and transition, moving from one state to another. The significance of the dividing line represents the equality in us all. From chaos, we once more create order. From order, we learn to understand and accept perspectives. From this perspective, we create more choices. From choices, we make progress. From progression, we evolve. Life once more has the opportunity to continue, even after death.

The colours are also significant. Gold has many meanings, but it is a symbol of wealth and prosperity. Power and luxury identify with royalty and nobility, including Divinity. Resistant to tarnish, it embodies timelessness and immortality. Its warm hue evokes the sun's positivity and healing energy. In alchemy, gold represents transformational power and spiritual perfection. People connect love with gold in union ceremony rings. It shows a commitment to symbolise a lasting relationship. In respect of all this, gold suggests the intense energy of the Universe. It is a colour that is pure. No other element can overshadow it. This also represents the colour of Archangel Uriel through her Universal ways.

Blue suggests a feeling of calmness and serenity through a tranquil aura. It advocates trust when relying upon the excellent character of professionalism in business. It also symbolises clarity of thought, effective communication, and sacred intuitive wisdom. Yet despite these positive aspects, it also holds negative ones. Blue captures emotions such as feelings of sadness or melancholy. This also represents the colour of Archangel Michael through his Universal ways.

Archangel Uriel and Archangel Michael are Angelic Universal twins. Individuals most often recognise Archangel Michael as a symbol of protection and courage. He is a warrior leading Divine forces against negativity in all its forms. Individuals turn to Michael for his guidance and strength during challenging times. His twin is Archangel Uriel. a bright, wise presence who shares her wisdom with us. A guardian of the Earth, she oversees and maintains order in the physical realms. Uriel promotes balance and enlightenment. Together, these Archangels associate harmony with peace. They bring order and understanding to chaos. Through them, they guide our intuition to what is right and wrong.

Each symbol has a set of lines representing the numbers 4, 3, and 1. I created this Unity symbol to assist in restoring order from chaos. Number 4 creates a foundation due to its links with the four corners or sides. It often signifies order and contributes to the balance of the world. The number 3 represents our completeness when accepting Divine perfection. When we achieve this, we can also create harmony and balance. To achieve balance, you must understand the connection between all these elements. The need for power and greed disrupted Universal Law, creating a catastrophic imbalance. To rectify this, it is down to you to dissect and comprehend these elements from your perspective. Number 1 signifies the unity of us all so we can create a new beginning for all. The commencement of this new journey demonstrates the connection between everything and everyone. To find peace and harmony, analyse and understand your situation. Then, make the necessary changes.

Index of Content

The Universe thought life would be an exciting adventure experienced through your senses. It's comparable to possessing an enchanted compass within your mind. It aims to help you navigate life's challenges by trusting your intuition. You lost the knowledge of using it at some point in your ancestral lineage.

From today, we will embark on a quest to rediscover it again.

Allow me to introduce Luci, my spiritual guide. To safeguard his energy, I've opted to alter his name. He was a respected actor in his time. People knew him for his rebellious behaviour and unconventional lifestyle. Despite his brief life, he imparted valuable lessons through his visionary entertainment. On our journey, we faced challenges and still disagree today, often because of my ego. Even so, we have a profound love for one another that will remain strong.

Hello! I'm Luci!

This book shows how I grew, from learning about karma to gaining deep wisdom. I'll share essential moments of heartache and powerful insights. These little things have changed how I see myself, my spirituality, and my intuition. You'll also see pictures of Luci, and we will help you understand the book.

Your intuition is that little voice inside your head. Sometimes, you feel something in your gut without any clear reason why. Your intuition provides valuable information that feels right but needs a clear source. Picture it as a wise and caring guide who knows you better than anyone else and only wants the best for you. This guide can help you with problems and solutions for decisions that may need time to solve. Many accomplished individuals favour trusting in this type of thought process. Some call it their sixth sense and use it to find resonance in decision-making.

Empathic guidance means understanding and empathising with emotions, connecting, and appreciating others' experiences. It's like wearing emotional glasses that let you see the world from someone else's view. This skill is excellent for making connections and showing care and help to others. You can improve your well-being and others' by connecting more with the world.

We all have natural gifts, like intuition and empathic guidance, in different amounts. We can better understand ourselves and others by developing and trusting these skills. Consider these your ultimate superpowers by embracing and harnessing these inherent gifts.

Recognising personal and professional obstacles is facing challenges on your path to success. Fear not; you're going to confront them with a positive mindset! Always trust your gut. Your emotions are forming a strong bond with someone. You must pay attention and not ignore or overlook it. Trusting your intuition and empathy will guide you on this fantastic life journey.

Finding Clarity on Life Purpose and Goals

To understand your life's purpose, reflect and explore. Trusting your instincts and empathy is essential during this transformative process. Find a quiet place and set aside time for this. Take slow breaths to calm your mind and focus on the present moment.

To feel grounded, consider your past experiences, achievements, and moments of joy. Your reflections can show what you care about, like what you're good at and passionate about. You need to know yourself well to make a difference in the world.

Journaling is a powerful tool that can help you in this self-discovery process. Put your thoughts and feelings onto paper. You gain clarity and understanding from insight into your inner world. You can embrace a new way of thinking and learning. It will give you a tangible record of your journey.

Listening to your intuition is another crucial aspect of this transformative journey. Always listen to your gut and that little voice, even if it goes against what you usually think. To enhance your intuitive thinking, try engaging in meditation. These techniques to connect with your inner wisdom will help you learn what is important to you.

Cultivate empathy towards yourself by treating yourself with kindness and compassion. Reflect on your experiences and emotions to take care of and love yourself. Treat yourself to small luxuries like a spa day, a favourite dessert, or a relaxing bath. These allow you to consider your aspirations and the fears hindering your progress. Take a moment to think about your values and beliefs. See how they affect your actions every day. Identify any moral principles that you want to prioritise in your life.

Having meaningful conversations with people from different backgrounds helps you understand their feelings. Listen to their stories, challenges, and triumphs. Try to understand their feelings and points of view. Reading enables you to understand the essential things in life. You will learn and understand your goals.

First, think about yourself and understand your feelings. Then, set clear goals that align with your values and interests. Break big goals into small steps to make a plan for achieving them. Write a brief mission statement about your goals and how you want to make a positive difference.

Remembering your life purpose and goals is an ongoing, ever-changing process. Make it a habit to revisit them to ensure they still align with your values. Stay open to changes. View them as chances to grow and adapt to fulfilling your purpose.

When I was young, I often wondered about the meaning of my life. I felt like the future I imagined didn't have the love I wanted. I worried about the uncertain future, consuming my thoughts. At forty-five, I began my spiritual journey. I started writing in a journal and distancing myself from specific individuals. This decision made me think, so I used the tarot cards I bought. With the support of an aware friend, I embarked on this path.

As I became more in touch with my intuition, I tried different tarot cards and started sensing things. I struggled to understand them and felt they should be more adaptable for me to comprehend. I purchased my first set of Angel Oracle cards. My belief in Archangels had always been steadfast, and these cards opened up a new world for me.

I got more decks, read for loved ones, and started a social media page to broaden my knowledge. I gave daily readings and accepted donations for personal consultations. I contacted the Universe, asking for money to continue my education in this field. The next day, I found a company on social media. They were offering half-price spiritual courses online. This turning point transformed everything!

During the pandemic, I signed up for three courses. I didn't stop there, though. In two years, I finished ten studies. It opened a new world, introducing me to Reiki and the Angelic realms. I attended online workshops and made new friends who share my spiritual beliefs. I still struggled with self-doubt. Over time, I saw evidence from others I had assisted. Trusting the process is necessary. With trust, you can prepare for future changes.

Reading cards for guidance has become a journey that transforms me, focused on love. This incredible journey has brought us joy as we experience and give love. On my path, I've been fortunate to help many people let go of negative energy from their past lives. I helped them explore their past lives and understand the meaning behind them. With my advice and support, they've overcome their challenges. It has given them the confidence to make good decisions and find their true purpose. Due to this, these individuals have transitioned from clients to close friends.

I wanted to go to more spiritual workshops. I needed help getting into a year-long Mentorship course. At that moment, I was unaware of the Universe's alternate intentions for my journey. I felt let down when I couldn't join the Mentorship, even though I attended two workshops before. Months later, I enrolled on a yearlong Angelic course. It helped me feel more enlightened and purposeful. There are always reasons behind what is and is not meant for us. I have no regrets because it has enriched my path.

I learned that education is only sometimes about gaining all knowledge. It's about focusing on what's essential for your specific job or career. Our perception of time is different from Universal Time because of tight deadlines. We often blame ourselves for not reaching goals or slowing progress. We need more time or missed an opportunity. Planning for the future is bright, but living in the present brings many chances to achieve goals.

Finding your true purpose makes you feel empowered. It also helps others and connects you to your intuition and empathy. You will embark on a personal and gratifying journey. This journey enables you to discover yourself and learn about a purposeful life.

Discovering your life purpose and goals is a personal and ongoing journey. It requires being open and honest with yourself. Trust your instincts, empathise with others, and practise self-care. This journey will help you find meaning and live a fulfilling life that aligns with your true self.

Answer the questions to discover different aspects of your meaningful journey. These questions cover topics such as self-care and goal setting. Change can help you grow. Start your journey by being open-hearted to explore your inner self.

How can you improve self-reflection and find your life purpose in your daily routine?

Have any experiences or achievements shaped your sense of purpose and values? What have you learned from these experiences?

How can you make a calming and focused space for thinking and self-exploration?

What self-care and self-love practice do you connect with? How can they help you discover yourself?

What goals are important to you and why?

When you think about finding your life purpose, how do you feel?

How do you imagine your journey will fulfil your life purpose and make a positive impact?

How can you turn big goals into small steps to make a plan to achieve them?

How can looking back at your goals and dreams help you stay true to your beliefs?

Identifying Personal and Professional Barriers

Often, we encounter personal challenges that could be dependent on our mindset. It can include emotional upbringing, deep-seated beliefs, and established routines. Lacking confidence or fear of risks can hold you back from reaching your potential. Procrastination, doubting oneself, and negative thoughts can hinder personal growth and achievement.

Professional barriers encompass external factors that may disrupt your well-being. It can impede your workplace, career growth and personal life. These obstacles can vary depending on circumstances, including restricted access to dependent resources. It can hold you back if you don't have chances, contacts, or training in your desired field.

My mother and I went to different churches in my late teens to learn about spirituality. I faced similar obstacles then. During this time, a psychic sent me two mysterious messages that interested me. The initial message implied that I would receive a house offer and have a strong intuitive sense of it. The second message hinted at a possible move to Scotland, with that same intuitive sense. I needed to clarify these messages, as I had not considered either. I only realised their importance once I had a spiritual awakening at forty-five.

I found out about the house offer when I got a council house. Yet, I couldn't afford a home or support myself due to my low income of £60 per week. This dream fell apart.

The second message informed me of the move to Scotland. Later, leaving my past behind for a fresh start led me to move there while I sought a job. But, after only five days, I realised I couldn't escape my inner struggles. So, I begged my friends to take me back home, and they did.

I came to understand that these messages taught me to value my self-worth. I realised that escaping from oneself only leads to carrying one's issues. Even though I knew about spiritualism, I still needed to improve my intuitive skills. I thought I knew better, and this belief persisted until that pivotal moment.

Understanding the process is not easy, but it is rewarding and freeing. It empowers you to step into your superpower as you realise your purpose in life. Like many others, your goal will involve helping others in your unique way. Have faith in your journey; the Universe will not desire to see you in distress. It aims to see you fulfil your purpose. Life isn't unfolding against you; it's evolving in your favour.

Overcoming personal barriers is essential to enhancing self-awareness. Remain determined to bring about positive transformation by acknowledging your obstacles. By setting achievable goals, you can build self-confidence. Challenging pessimistic thoughts by venting them through expressive writing is also helpful. Additionally, do not hesitate to seek support and advice from those you trust. Their support can provide valuable advice and motivation to overcome your obstacles.

You can address professional barriers by adopting an initiative-taking stance. Identify your problems and brainstorm ideas to solve them. You can connect with coworkers or industry experts and learn more about your field.

Remember that everyone encounters barriers at various points, which is normal. The crucial factor is to maintain a positive growth mindset and remain persistent. Do not let the first obstacle discourage you. Each experience is an opportunity to learn. You can overcome these challenges with determination and a robust support system. You will soon realise that your intuition and empathy are helping you succeed in life.

The following questions serve as a self-reflection exercise. You are understanding the barriers that affect your life. Take the time to answer these questions and be honest in your responses.

What self-limiting beliefs or negative thought patterns are hindering your progress?

Do you often procrastinate, and if so, what triggers this behaviour?

Are you aware of recurring self-doubt or lacking confidence in certain areas?

Do you have any habits or routines holding you back from growing?

How do you react to failure or setbacks? Do you engage in negative self-talk during these times?

What external factors or circumstances are currently affecting your professional growth and well-being?

Do you need access to resources or opportunities necessary for your career advancement?

Do you have a solid professional network, or do gaps in your connections need attention?

Do you feel like something you don't know is holding you back in your field? What steps can you take to overcome this?

Have you encountered any workplace activities or issues discouraging your professional development?

To build trust in your instincts, recognise and embrace your inner wisdom. Your gut feelings and hunches are your mind's way of guiding you in the right direction. The initial step involves being attentive to them. It's essential to understand that, on occasion, they immediately appear logical. It's acceptable, especially as you are in the learning phase. Allow yourself to grow by nurturing these gifts. You may doubt yourself sometimes, but give yourself a chance to grow and improve. Your subconscious is still working on strange information. Your intuition will provide you with helpful ideas to overcome this.

To practice intuition, ask a fundamental question with a "yes" or "no" response. For instance, you could ask, "Should I get the red coat?" Allow the Universe to respond with a clear signal. A dog could represent "yes," while a cat signifies "no." It It would be best to remain aware of your surroundings, so be patient during this process.

When I first saw Luci, it was hard to recognise who he was because he was so important. I subjected him to daily tests to confirm his existence. Once, I wanted a rubber duck. I found many rubber ducks at a big store, which made me more sure. Since then, I've associated Luci with a frog. Even now, seeing a frog daily reminds me that he is still here and helping.

Once you see your answer come true, you will know for sure. To get better, ask more complex questions and use unusual symbols to trust your intuition.

Think about times in the past when your instincts were correct so you can trust them more. Think back to the times when you had good experiences. Those memories can help you trust your intuition. Remember when you disregarded your intuition, and things went off track? They will both remind you always to trust your intuitive gut instincts.

Trusting your intuition is the same as nurturing a friendship only with yourself. You will feel more connected to yourself as you listen to and trust your inner voice. Be with open-minded, supportive people who appreciate your intuition. Please share your thoughts and feelings with them. Listen to their experiences in return. You can create a supportive environment. It boosts confidence and trust in yourself.

Please invest the necessary time to respond to the following questions. Being honest with yourself will improve your understanding of your intuition.

How do you currently view the process of developing trust in your intuition? Are you being patient with yourself?

What steps can you take to maintain an open mind and enjoy embracing your intuition?

Has your intuition played a significant role in your decision-making? In what situations? What did you learn from it?

Have there been instances where you ignored your intuition? In hindsight, would it have been beneficial for you to listen?

Has your intuition played a significant role in your decision-making? In what situations?

Do you notice any patterns or themes you can learn from in your intuition?

Have you ever asked a simple question and received a straightforward, intuitive answer?

Do you have people who can value and encourage your intuition? How can you engage with them more?

How do you form a group of helpful, understanding people who can share their instincts?

Exploring Energy Healing Techniques for Self-Nurturing

Energy healing involves rebalancing your chakras to enhance physical, emotional, and intuitive well-being. Even without much evidence, people enjoy using these self-care techniques. To nurture yourself:

- Approach energy healing methods with an open mind.

- Recognise them as traditional and complementary alternatives to rejuvenating your health.

- Learn energy healing techniques to improve your well-being through empathy and intuition.

These energy techniques can assist you in discovering balance and concentration in your life.

- Reiki is a Japanese energy healing technique. Practitioners heal by touching or holding their hands above specific body areas. They channel healing energy. Recipients stay clothed for accessibility and comfort. Practitioners rely on intuition and empathy to identify and correct energy imbalances. This process enhances emotional well-being and mental clarity.

- Chakra Healing balances the body's energy centres. These centres are like spinning wheels. Achieving balance in these chakras is crucial for energy healing. Intuitive empathy can help identify blockages or excess activity. You can use various methods to harmonise these energy centres.

- Crystal Healing has been an energy practice for centuries despite limited scientific evidence. Trust your intuition when choosing crystals that align with your energy or intentions. When placed on or around your body, they can help promote energy balance.

- For thousands of years, people have used meditation for different reasons. It helps with relaxation, stress, and finding inner guidance. To achieve mental clarity and emotional peace, train your mind to focus on one thing at a time. Select techniques that align with your goals. It can help you embark on a meaningful personal journey.

- Aromatherapy harnesses the power of essential oils and concentrated extracts from aromatic plants. The oils impact your body's energy and emotions by fostering soothing self-care. When using oils on your skin, choose good quality ones and dilute them since they can be intense. Trust your intuition when picking oils that connect with you. Diffusing them can elevate your mood and boost mental alertness. Adding some essential oil to a warm bath and inhaling the steam allows you to relax and feel refreshed.

In conclusion, these energy healing techniques are valuable for self-care and self-nurturing practices. Talk to an expert or research before starting aromatherapy or any energy healing. The outcomes may vary from person to person. It's important to remember that energy healing techniques can't replace medical care. See your doctor or healthcare professional for guidance if you have health concerns.

Consider the following questions as a guiding compass. Each one aids you in reflecting on your preferences, comfort level, and intentions. They will help you find the practices that suit your needs and goals for your well-being journey.

Do you feel comfortable with alternative and complementary approaches to nurturing your well-being?

What specific goals do you have when considering using energy-healing techniques?

Which would you prefer and why? Reiki or techniques that involve visualisation and intuitive empathy, like Chakra Healing?

How much do you value your intuition when choosing crystals for energy healing?

In what ways do you believe meditation can contribute to your self-care routine? How comfortable are you with exploring different techniques to align with your intentions?

Do you like using essential oils to make a relaxing, self-care environment? Can you trust your intuition when selecting oils that resonate with you?

Do you like using essential oils for a calm self-care space? How can you make sure these practices improve your health?

If you're new to energy healing, how will you research a safe and effective method?

Creating a Mental and Emotional Self-Care Routine

Prioritising your mental and emotional health is essential in our busy world. By practising, you can get healthier and better at dealing with life's challenges. Caring for your well-being is not a luxury. People often overlook or set aside it in favour of prioritising the needs of others. Taking care of yourself helps you handle life's challenges better. This form of self-control manages stress and fosters emotional resilience. It, in turn, contributes to a happier and more fulfilling life. How you act during a demonstration affects how well you handle tough times.

Establishing boundaries is crucial to being healthy and having good relationships. Boundaries are like invisible lines that determine what you find acceptable and comfortable. They apply to different situations and interactions. Clear, respectful boundaries help communicate your needs, limits, and values. These can further nurture fulfilling relationships while maintaining integrity. When you embrace this empowering approach, you protect your emotional and mental well-being. It reduces the risk of burnout. You also enhance your ability to form more profound and meaningful connections. Clear boundaries in relationships create respect, trust, and balance when giving and receiving. When you set limits for self-care, it helps you focus on yourself and prevents guilt or stress.

Setting and keeping healthy boundaries is a crucial way to love and respect yourself. Below, you will find different ways to care for your mind and emotions. You are assessing and acknowledging your current mental and emotional state. To improve your health, focus on eating well, exercising and getting enough sleep. You are dividing time daily to disconnect from screens, social media, and news updates. Taking a break outdoors helps reduce stress and information overload. Continuous learning and skill development are vital for personal and professional growth. Pursuing career goals advances your path and can enhance self-esteem for positive well-being.

Changing your self-care routine is essential as your needs change for a better life. Flexibility helps you handle challenges and unexpected changes, promoting personal growth.

Remember, self-care varies from person to person. To have good practice, adjust your routine to match what you like and what's happening around you. Be patient yet consistent. If you have trouble sticking to a routine, ask a therapist for help.

They can guide you and keep you accountable. Think about what stresses you out and what triggers have affected your emotions.

What emotions do you feel, and how can understanding them help you care for yourself?

Can you identify any specific stressors or triggers affecting your emotional well-being?

What realistic and achievable goals can you set for a self-care routine?

Do these goals align with what you want, such as reducing stress or boosting self-esteem?

Do you practice mindfulness, deep breathing, or muscle relaxation?

Are there other ways to improve your mental and emotional health and handle stress?

Are you open to exploring mind-body practices like Yoga or Tai Chi to reduce stress triggers? How do you envision these practices fitting into your self-care regimen?

How can you fit exercise into a routine to increase your mood and reduce stress?

Are you eating a balanced diet with vegetables and fruits to nourish your body and emotions?

How can you ensure enough sleep to support your emotional well-being and health?

How often do you divide time in your daily routine to disconnect from screens and the digital world?

What outdoor activities or nature experiences most restore your balance and tranquillity?

Do you notice changes in your stress when you take breaks from news and social media?

How do you improve your skills in both your personal and professional life? What impact can/do these activities have on your well-being?

What are your career goals, and how are you working toward achieving them? How does this pursuit contribute to your self-esteem and sense of well-being?

How can you grow and feel happier? What steps are you willing to take to make this a reality?

Cultivating Resilience and Self-Compassion

Nurturing resilience and self-compassion are essential skills that help you overcome life's challenges. It fosters a more optimistic and self-assured relationship with yourself. Begin with self-awareness and allow for an understanding of your thoughts and emotions. Keep practising deep breathing and meditation to improve emotional awareness. You can mentally reframe challenges as opportunities for personal growth.

To overcome challenges, improve your critical thinking skills and practice self-kindness. Being kind to yourself helps you become stronger and more confident. Yet, it takes time and patience. Embrace change by saying 'no' when facing overwhelming challenges. Seeking tailored support can be beneficial.

We all experience pain, failure, and imperfections. It makes us all connected as humans. It enables you to embrace your emotions without passing judgment on yourself. When you celebrate small successes, you feel more confident and motivated. Focus on the positive attributes of your journey.

How does resilience and self-compassion enhance your self-assured and optimistic self-relationship?

How does self-awareness influence your ability to comprehend and conquer life's challenges?

How can you turn challenges into chances to grow by being more positive?

How have you improved your ability to think and handle challenges? Do you maintain balance by being both kind and compassionate to yourself in the process?

How can you accept change and say 'no' when you have too much to do? What strategies have you found effective in these situations?

Why is it important to acknowledge that making mistakes is part of being human? How has self-compassion helped you cope with your imperfections?

How does it make you feel when you realise that we all face similar challenges and come together as a community?

How do you celebrate your successes, no matter how small? Does this practice impact your confidence and motivation in achieving your goals?

How do you foster self-compassion in your daily life? Has it contributed to a more resilient, confident, and strong sense of self?

Understanding the Impact of Past Experiences when Making Decisions

We must trust our instincts and understand others to see how our past affects our choices. Intuition means making decisions without using logic to think about someone or something. It examines how past experiences have influenced you, especially with certain conditions. You'll discover hidden patterns and connections that have developed from these events. Empathy is when you imagine how someone feels and see things from their perspective. Remember, you're not supporting their actions. Instead, you're understanding the situation better.

For example, suppose you face repeated failures in a specific area of your life. Your intuition might tell you to be more careful or suggest a different approach. Positive experiences can give you confidence, helping you move forward with purpose. The knowledge you gain will serve as a guiding force in trusting your decision-making.

This process teaches you to trust your intuition and be kind in future projects. The more attuned you are, the more attuned you'll be to those who shy away from challenges due to past failures.

Imagine a manager who knows how an employee feels about being a leader. They wonder if their ability to handle this role is due to past overwhelming experiences. The manager's observation should be enough to recognise and address these concerns. The decision to support the employee and the company helps both of them.

When you combine intuition with empathy, you make better decisions. Delving into past experiences creates a new level of understanding. You're allowing yourself to see beyond concealed motivations or attachments. You'll understand the weight of these burdens and find ways to release them. You can help others make decisions and feel empowered by customising your advice.

Identifying and Addressing Self-Doubt Triggers

To feel better, start a journey to overcome self-doubt and regret. To navigate this path well, you need to identify and address the things that make you doubt yourself. These are the specific situations where self-doubt starts. When you doubt yourself, there are three harmful thought patterns. They are trying to be perfect, comparing yourself to others, and feeling regret. Addressing these detrimental patterns is paramount. Being proactive boosts your confidence, resilience, and satisfaction in life.

Empowering yourself in this journey involves understanding the contributing elements. When encompassing uncertainties or regrets, you liberate yourself from their constraining grip. One way to discover more about yourself is by keeping a journal and writing down times when you feel unsure. This practice helps you understand what causes these feelings. It lets your thoughts and emotions come out. Engaging in this reflective practice establishes the groundwork for a more profound comprehension. The idea that irrational fears can affect outcomes may or may not come true. Let your intuition guide you on the steps to overcome moments of uncertainty.

Cultivating self-awareness is another step in conquering self-doubt. Recognising and challenging thought patterns allows you to tune into your emotions. By discerning when and where self-doubt emerges, you can address it. Self-doubt is a common emotional obstacle. It manifests through negative thought patterns eroding self-esteem and confidence. Consider where your lack of conviction stems. Often, it can come from specific situations or people, as it can impact various aspects of your life.

Trying to maintain a perfect life is the relentless pursuit of lawlessness. The fear of making a big mistake or failing to meet high standards can paralyse you. When self-doubt creeps in, you must remind yourself that nobody is perfect. Making mistakes is a natural part of your intuitive growth for learning. Rather than pursuing perfection, focus on continuous self-improvement as an ongoing journey.

Comparison is another toxic thought pattern that intensifies self-doubt. It involves comparing yourself to others, especially those with similarities. Limit exposure to such triggers and focus on your progress and growth.

Remember that everyone has a unique journey with strengths and weaknesses. Rather than comparing yourself to others, appreciate and celebrate your achievements. When you succeed, your confidence grows, and people notice your unique qualities.

Regret is a natural emotion and holds the potential to be a valuable teacher. Instead of dwelling on past mistakes, reflect on them and learn valuable lessons. Turning regret into a catalyst for growth involves a deliberate process of introspection. We can learn from our regrets and use them to make better choices in the future.

Thinking about the worst things that could happen can make you too afraid to take risks or try new things. Challenge these exaggerated perceptions by seeking concrete evidence to support them. Reflect on past experiences to identify incidents contributing to speculative, undesirable outcomes. To better understand challenges, break down pessimistic scenarios. It builds confidence in achieving success.

Remember, overcoming self-doubt and regret is an ongoing process. Occasional moments of self-doubt are natural. You can have a happier life by practising and being kind to yourself.

I've faced many different situations. Most often connected to lessons I need to learn. I navigate through different experiences and relationships. These invaluable lessons have shaped many bad choices. Difficult situations have pushed me, and I trusted my ego more than my instincts. Looking back, I've realised that even though these situations were painful, they showed me how brave and strong I am. They helped me overcome the challenges I faced while I was awakening.

One poignant memory involves the sudden passing of my dog. I felt our time was ending, but I didn't know when or how it would happen. Trying to predict could cause problems. It started with a routine vet check, revealing a heart murmur in a dog who had always boasted a strong heart. Scheduled for an X-ray a few days later, the turn of events was swift. They told me that they would have to euthanise him. I had 30 minutes to come back after the check-up. The devastation was profound, resonating with fellow pet lovers. I spent some time with him and said goodbye.

I felt terrible. It was to be another repeated karmic lesson from my early teens.

I followed the Universe's guidance, even though I didn't understand some tasks. The loss made me feel confused. The next day, I felt immense sadness that affected my concentration and emotions. Seeking clarity, I turned to herbal remedies. Yet, I didn't get the expected relief; the box fell, and even the tablet slipped from my mouth. Undeterred, I persisted. Within 20-30 minutes, my emotions took a turbulent turn. I felt frustrated and sad, so I blamed the Universe and Archangel Michael for the loss. The actual reason, obscured by the fear of loneliness, remained blocked. Overwhelmed, I contemplated ending my life, but I only had limited resources.

The next day, I felt guilty for what I had done, so I started meditating. Archangel Michael tapped the latest soul contract, a scroll against his leg. Unyielding, I stood firm, expressing my readiness to face whatever he had in store. In response, he laughed, bonked me on the head with the scroll, and inquired if I felt better. I affirmed my improved mindset in my meditative state, where I felt unshakeable.

Archangel Uriel, Archangel Michael's twin, came forward with my dog. She signalled that I needed to say goodbye because he had a mission to complete. Kneeling, I hugged and kissed him, uttering my final goodbyes. He turned into a young boy, approximately 3-4 years old, in a poignant transformation. He asked if I would be his "Mummy," despite being 48 years old and deeming it a stretch to be a mother, I agreed. I accepted his fate. Archangel Uriel gave me a gold paw print brooch pinned into my heart.

The initial pain was intense but fleeting. The boy turned away, disappearing along with Archangel Uriel. My meditation and understanding of my initial grief were over.

As I thought more, I realised that this experience helped me empathise with others. This unique gift took a few months to perfect.

Several months later, I gained insight into the identity of my dog. That being my spiritual guide, Luci. I found a picture from his childhood. He's holding a dog like mine. The little boy is in my meditation. The realisation was astounding. Luci's goal was to teach me about unconditional love, something I didn't know before. I now understand the idea of love. The sense of it empowers me. As other creative visionaries said, love is everywhere for those looking for it.

Are you ready to face your uncertainties and start growing? Consider the following questions to glean insights and wisdom from disappointing outcomes. They encourage you to reflect on your experiences and emotions. Let honesty guide you as you explore yourself, grow, and improve.

What specific actions or decisions led to a regrettable situation? How might other choices have influenced the outcome?

What makes you doubt yourself or feel regret? How might recognising them empower your personal growth?

How do perfectionism, comparison, and regret affect your self-confidence and well-being? How can you address these damaging thought patterns?

How can you become more aware of recurring patterns of self-doubt in your life? In what ways do these patterns influence different factors in your life?

How can you reduce the negative effect of comparing yourself to others? How can you shift your attention towards personal progress and growth?

Does imagining the worst outcome stop you from taking risks and trying new things? What strategies can you use to confront and disrupt these cognitive patterns?

What can you learn from your past mistakes, and how can you use them to make better choices in the future?

How does being kind to yourself help you overcome self-doubt and regret? What can you do to become stronger and better at handling these challenges?

Everyone is on a distinctive path, equipped with unique strengths and weaknesses. How does your perspective impact how you see your worth and growth compared to others?

Understanding and letting go of difficult experiences can be a delicate process. It entails maintaining a compassionate perspective on all the factors involved. Being prepared to express your feelings makes you feel supported in various ways.

There are different approaches that you can consider for emotional healing. You can talk to people you trust and listen to others who have been through the same experiences as you. To increase your creativity, you can write in a journal, send letters, or do art to heal.

Establishing a secure, non-judgmental environment to navigate past traumas is crucial. If the situation is serious, ask for help from a mental and emotional health professional. Active listening allows them to devote their complete and undivided attention to you. Their guidance can encourage you to feel at ease as you recall past thoughts and emotions.

One of my earlier traumatic experiences was when my grandmother fell ill. I had purchased a Bible searching for a purpose, sensing that there was something more to my life. I read the Bible each night, praying for 'God' to save her. But one night, I was too tired to pray, and the next day, she died. This loss left me traumatised, as it was my first encounter with death and the intense love I held for her.

This sorrow pushed me to delve further into the religion for the next three years. Instead of finding solace or understanding, I continued on a downward spiral. I began accepting low-paying jobs and struggling with self-worth to please others. I also endured relationships that brought me physical, mental, and emotional pain. I lacked guidance, relying on my ego, which I found challenging to trust. I embarked on a lengthy journey of repeated karmic lessons, one after another.

Karmic lessons are painful

It took me a while to become more intuitive. I had to understand, learn from, and let go of these lessons from the past. I now recognise that everything happens for a reason, and my purpose was clear. I share what I've learned from life so others can find their purpose, too.

As you look inward, think about your experiences and specific memories. Your emotions serve as a lens which heightens your awareness of all that has transpired. Acknowledging the different situations will support how these experiences have influenced your thoughts. If you were not prepared, you couldn't analyse these repeating patterns.

By going through this process, you can develop a positive understanding. It involves forgiving yourself and healing. You will know the signs when you face a situation that could be traumatic. You will learn the essential ideas, causes, or links related to previous events. Your instincts will guide how you react to other people's negativity. To stay present, try practising mindfulness through meditation or deep breathing exercises. It will help you deal with the situation better.

You can trust your intuition by acquiring your newfound inner strength and resilience. By visualising potential outcomes, you can avoid feeling overwhelmed or emotional. Engaging in this process, you'll reframe your perception of the potential trauma. You can expose yourself by learning how to handle the situation better.

Identifying, releasing, and healing traumatic experiences is always a difficult journey. To create a caring environment, combine self-awareness, intuition, and empathy. Listen to your gut, change how you see things, and let understanding make you feel stronger.

As you acknowledge and release your painful experiences, ponder these questions. They will make you reflect and better understand your emotional healing. Approach them with an open mind.

How can you make a safe space for yourself when discussing your painful experiences?

What role does self-forgiveness play in healing your traumatic experiences?

Can repeating patterns and emotional reactions affect how you understand past traumas?

When should you consider seeking the help of a health professional to deal with your trauma?

How can you trust your gut feelings and make better choices after tough times?

How can you be more mindful in the present when dealing with traumatic situations?

How can empathy and intuition help you understand and release your traumatic experiences?

How can active listening and empathy contribute to your healing process?

What artistic endeavours would you consider to let go of past trauma?

Regrets left unaddressed can cast a heavy shadow on your thoughts and emotions. They hinder your ability to move forward and live your desired life. The persistent echo of past decisions can cloud the present if allowed to linger. Clinging to self-blame and guilt, rather than forgiving yourself, only prolongs your suffering. If you don't deal with regrets, they can hold you back from enjoying the present and creating a better future. If your regrets involve others, consider reaching out and offering apologies if appropriate. In cases where this isn't possible, write a letter with the intent to provide closure. If you choose not to send it, burn it to help you find peace within your conflicted mind.

Regret, often viewed as a source of pain, holds the potential to become your most profound teacher in life. Reflecting on and learning from your past errors turns regret into valuable wisdom. It empowers you to pave the way for self-improvement and emotional healing. To let go of the past, look inward. It helps you understand why you feel regret.

Dwelling on the past can hinder your enjoyment of the present moment. Utilising it as a tool for reflection can lead to a deeper understanding. Remain mindful of the circumstances that drove your past choices. You can unravel valuable insights into why you made those decisions at the time. This process liberates you from guilt, fostering personal growth, resilience, and inner peace. When you see regret as an important lesson, it can help you make better choices.

This profession has brought forth a significant sense of regret and guilt. It all stemmed from not surrendering to my initial calling during my late teens. Starting on this path sooner might have lessened the suffering of others. It still lingers. It's common to feel remorse. It's essential to start pursuing your true passion when you're young to grow as a person and in your career. Every person's journey is different, and the time it takes to find your true calling can vary. Understanding emotions, thoughts, and instincts in different situations is essential.

Everyone's purpose is essential

Your journey is unique. Finding your true purpose adds depth to personal and professional development.

To better understand, I researched, meditated, and sought advice from mentors. I now know that my current actions bear more significance and value than in my late teens. Despite the challenges, I've discerned the reasons behind many aspects of my life. Every experience, positive or negative, has contributed to my understanding. My ability helps more individuals navigate their journeys. I am aligning them to their calling only when they are ready.

Past energy healers and psychic mediums offer opportunities to learn about spirituality. Some people still associate the new age movement with occultists or devil worshippers. Seeing that more people accept spiritualism and energy healing is excellent. I see it as an 'emotional and intuitive understanding' to remove the stigma, but these are labels. In this climate, you can now become aware that we all have the potential to impact people's lives. We all can help each other navigate the complexities of relationships and situations. We value learning, personal growth, and trusting our intuition. Divine guidance is valuable in everything we do.

Some people take advantage of others' desperation. They are selling spells and magic to "help" them. The intention is to extract their money and leave them in even greater despair and needing more. These aspects are not confined to spiritual crafts but also to corporate marketing. Companies use terms like 'transformation', 'sustainability' and 'commitment.' It's intended to create positive change through culture selling. These words lose meaning without real action. Especially people who use persuasive language, Tarot or Oracle cards, and energy healing. Anyone who utilises specific terms gains your trust and money.

Consistency is critical to determine someone's reliability, even though many people are sincere. When assessing them, consider their past performance. Above all, trust your empathetic intuition. Your heightened senses are your gifts from the Universe as it lacks a physical body. Embrace and hone these gifts through your intuitive and empathic actions. Wield them, as they hold tremendous power in your goals.

Accepting your calling is always possible, regardless of any criteria. It's an opportunity to impact your life and the world. Your past experiences and challenges will help you provide valuable help to others.

In essence, questioning and experiencing everything is crucial for comprehending events and experiences. Stay true to your values and beliefs, and follow the right path. This approach enables personal growth, benefitting yourself and those around you. Each experience becomes a building block on your way to self-improvement.

Talking to a trusted person can help you feel better and more confident. It provides emotional support, enabling you to make up for past mistakes. Learning from the past and addressing regrets takes time, patience, and effort.

It's now time to channel your energy into constructive action. The following questions can serve as prompts for continuous self-reflection and self-improvement. You can navigate towards healing regrets and gaining wisdom from past mistakes. With persistent self-compassion, you can move forward. Each day will always present an opportunity to make better choices. Success in achieving your quest for personal growth and inner peace is attainable. It's important to remember that this journey should unfold. The lessons learned along the way can prove invaluable to you.

Are there any past regrets or mistakes that make it difficult for you to move forward?

How can forgiving yourself for mistakes help with your emotional healing and well-being?

How can you transform regrets into a chance to learn, become strong, and find peace? Have you considered reaching out to those involved to deepen your understanding?

What caused you to make choices in the past that you now regret? How can understanding these factors help you grow and learn more about yourself?

Have you considered apologising to people to show more understanding? What obstacles could prevent you? How can you overcome these challenges?

How do you see the value of confiding in a trusted friend and sharing your inner thoughts? Can this provide emotional support and guide your actions to prevent future regrets?

How can you believe personal growth and inner peace are ongoing journey?

To find your dreams and interests, trust your instincts and understand your emotions. You ignored these things for personal reasons. But now, your awakening will help you know your purpose. It's a transformative process as you identify your strengths, weaknesses, fears and desires. When you explore why you do things, you will see patterns in your thoughts and actions. You can find the areas that need improvement to be true to yourself.

Now is the moment to open your mind and see the world!

Trusting your gut and understanding others' feelings boosts your confidence and personal growth. These principles are the guiding lights that shape your conduct and actions. You can feel aligned and at peace when you reconnect with your core values. This alignment helps you find and set goals that give your life purpose. It resonates with your passions and the perceived impact you'll have on the world. When you understand something, you can make thoughtful decisions. Explore and align with them so your choices will continue to lead to a more fulfilling life.

This journey is fostering a deeper understanding of your purpose. Continue your mindful and emotional practices with journaling and meditation. Share your thoughts and feelings with others to improve your values and beliefs. Self-discovery is paving the way to continued evolution.

To discover your potential, explore your values, beliefs, and emotions. Insight gathered from the emotional values opens the gateway to potential achievements. Your understanding provides clarity of your true desires and sources of motivation. Often, we chastise ourselves for missing deadlines because we have missed the opportunity. That isn't so.

Many people have told me they felt me in their dreams, during meditation, or through intuition. Some are unaware that it's me offering this support, and that's fine. I'm not doing it for personal satisfaction. I'm doing it because it's my purpose. I care and love them, even though I do not know them. It's good to know that my work helps people who need it. Love is a beautiful and valuable gift that we should all cherish.

Healing distressing situations is hard when I don't know the people or location. I no longer question the requests of the Universe and my Archangels. It can happen at any time of day, more often at night, no matter where I am. Sometimes, empathetic people can feel my pain and support me as I heal.

I've transcended my many pasts and past life regrets, guilt, and the judgment of others. I've gained so much invaluable insight since answering my awakening. I've unlearned many things I once thought proper. I am breaking away from conventional beliefs that no longer serve me. I can sit with someone, think of them, and help ease their pain. It gives them a moment of relief and allows them to open up. It lets them tune into their intuitive thoughts to understand their experiences better. It empowers them to move forward in a direction that befits them.

Caring is loving unconditionally

To realise the importance of unlocking your true potential, answer the following questions. When discovering how to become your best self, you can tackle the challenges holding you back. The more you explore, the more you understand how these things shape your purpose. You'll make better choices that match your values and start to see a future-filled meaning. Stay on this path of self-discovery to keep improving.

Do personal values, beliefs, and emotions help you reach your full potential?

How can knowing what you value help you achieve your life's purpose?

What reasons could make you hide your desires, passions, and emotions? How can you overcome these barriers?

How can you align your actions with your core values and beliefs?

Has your gut ever guided you to make a significant choice or learn something new about yourself?

How can talking to people who think like you help you evolve and learn about yourself?

How can your life become more meaningful as you grow and explore yourself?

By developing a growth mindset, you can learn from past experiences. Extracting wisdom from these moments can turn them into steps for personal development. Evolving through dedicated learning and self-reflection is crucial. This transformative journey depends on your willingness to examine past adversities. Identify any triggers that lead to self-doubt and regrets. Embrace these principles. They'll open the door to a mindset that thrives on new challenges. You can place a high value on your resilience.

To grow and improve, you need courage to face your past. It involves identifying historic regrets and mistakes that linger in your conscience. It anchors you in the present, affecting various aspects of your life. These include relationships, career choices, educational pursuits, and personal decisions. You can start a journey to a better future by recognising regret and mistakes. The things you learn from your past help you grow and develop.

It is important to remember that the human experience is imperfect. Every one of us, without exception, makes mistakes and carries regrets to some extent. Rather than letting self-blame overshadow your growth, embrace the healing power of self-compassion. Extend empathy and understanding to yourself during this phase of self-awareness. To grow as a person, it helps to have a kinder view of your judgments. To face challenges, you must be willing to step outside your comfort zone and confront them. Accept and learn from your regrets and mistakes to become kinder and wiser.

In moments of discomfort and uncertainty, actual development can flourish. Push yourself beyond what you think you can do; you'll discover new abilities. These experiences can be transformative. Expand your horizons and instil a profound sense of self-confidence. Venture beyond your comfort zone, and you cultivate a deep understanding of adaptability. Your ability to adopt a new mindset thrives on the excitement of positive progress. It opens an opportunity to unlock your full potential and undergo personal evolution.

Focus on what lies ahead. Shift your attention away from past regrets and mistakes. Identify areas where you wish to enhance your life. When self-doubt begins to cast its shadow, take an active stance. Challenge any remaining negative beliefs that threaten your confidence.

Remember to draw on the evidence of your past successes. The milestones you achieve are the progress you're making. These are reminders of your capabilities and the potential that you have.

This mindset leads to greater self-confidence and a more rewarding life. You construct a blueprint for how you want your life to unfold. To attract opportunities and helpful people, set goals and trust your instincts. Remain open to change and be receptive to the new opportunities this attracts. These all become pillars of strength during challenging times. All offer fresh perspectives, insights, and the motivation to persevere. Consider these questions to develop a growth mindset for the changes you will face. They'll unlock your potential for both personal and professional development.

How do you approach your past regrets and mistakes? Do you view them as opportunities for growth, or do they weigh on your present life?

Do you empathise with your past or blame and criticise yourself?

How do you challenge these thoughts when faced with self-doubt and negative beliefs?

How have you pushed beyond your comfort zone to confront challenges and uncertainties?

Have you learned a lesson from a mistake or regret that helped you grow?

Do you want to improve your skills or learn more in a specific area of your life?

Do you have a supportive network of friends, mentors, or colleagues? How have they influenced your development? Can these relationships further aid your progress?

How can you see your potential for improving and growing to be your best self?

Navigating Family Beliefs and Expectations

Understanding and dealing with family beliefs and expectations can be challenging yet meaningful. Although this journey might feel like a wild ride of emotions, it can help you gain personal strength. You are stepping into uncharted territory armed only with your intuition. Allow self-awareness to blossom by considering your beliefs, values, and dreams. Imagine it as unloading your present backpack to prepare for an extraordinary adventure. Preparation makes your journey smoother and less stressful. Explore the vast landscape of ethical principles. In it, seek only the gems that align with your true self.

Culture, society, and generation shape your family's beliefs and expectations. Your grandparents and parents may hold them in high regard, instilling a sense of duty in you to follow them. These beliefs can make you feel like you belong but might not match your values. Gaining yourself the freedom to explore your path without judgment is essential. Identify any conditioning that has shaped your beliefs and try to detach from them. A small step can lead to much personal growth and transformation.

Heartfelt conversations with your family are essential to understanding each other's values. Create a safe space for your decisions to align with these values and goals. Instead of doing what your family expects, choose a path that feels true to you. Change will not happen overnight, but establishing healthy boundaries is essential. It's saying, "This is me; this is you, and here's where we can meet." To build resilience, focus on what's essential and recharge your energy. Being true to yourself helps you stand out and keeps everyone's well-being intact.

Patience is your trusted companion as you navigate through your family's dynamics. It offers a fundamental solution to achieve harmony in your relationships. When ready, have an honest and open conversation with your family. Express your perspective and listen to their point of view, too. Making significant changes in your beliefs or behaviour can feel daunting. Consider making any gradual changes over time.

One of my personal stories begins with a strong desire for meaningful connections. It ended up surprising me in unexpected ways. As a peacemaker, I have always tended to prioritise others' happiness. I discovered that my efforts never led to the changes I hoped for, no matter what I said or did.

The reality of this became evident when it involved my own family. I had always been the one to make the trip to visit them. Various reasons made it difficult for them to travel to see me. One was that they resided in Scotland whilst I lived in the North of England.

I appreciate handwritten letters as they signify a genuine connection with others. Someone has taken the time to think about another person to share their life updates. I understand that we live in a digital era where we exchange information immediately. I also appreciate the sentiment of taking the time to write and read a letter. Text messages do not capture what needs expressing, especially when you're on the move.

Examine personal beliefs, family expectations, and balancing individuality with your interactions with family. Reflect on your values in family relationships by considering these questions.

What do you currently believe in, value, and dream about? Have you taken the time to explore and understand these aspects of your life?

Do you see any ways your family may have influenced your beliefs? How might separating yourself from these influences contribute to your personal growth?

Do you struggle to make choices that match your beliefs while staying close to your family?

How can you establish and discuss healthy limits with your family to ensure you are okay?

Have you ever found yourself prioritising others' happiness at your own expense?

Do you like writing and reading letters to connect with others, even in today's digital age?

How can you stay true to yourself and create harmony within your family?

How can you choose what you believe, even if it's not what your family expects?

Self-expression can offer you a secure and supportive environment for self-discovery. It allows you to tend to your needs when you find it challenging to get support from other sources. Add empathy to your writing. You'll understand your inner child's experiences better. Over time, you've carried the weight of these emotions alone. If you are afraid of judgment, speaking up, or hurting others, you will keep feeling the same way. When you heal your inner child, please keep an open mind as they share their feelings.

As you search for answers and healing, I'll share a personal story about the power of journaling. This story shows how writing can heal emotional wounds from the past. Unearthing concealed traumas led me to acknowledgement, emotional understanding, forgiveness, and liberation.

When I started writing in my journal, I faced my traumatic experiences for the first time. I wrote before bedtime, so I wasn't overthinking before sleep. I released a babble of words about all the memories that sprung to my mind. The earliest memory surfacing was an incident involving a family member. I would be around three years old and still reliant on a pacifier. I refused to speak. I cannot confirm the accuracy of my age during this recollection. I later understood that my mother was a narcissist and lied about my past.

This trusted person decided to perform a magic trick which required my pacifier. I was hesitant, but I trusted him and handed it to him. He concealed his hands behind his back before presenting them to me, palms held shut. He then asked me to guess which hand the pacifier was in. I tapped his right hand, feeling sure it was there. He slowly unveiled it (so it felt), and to my shock, the pacifier wasn't there. I tapped his other hand, and once again, he revealed an empty hand. I was so upset when I saw my pacifier disappear I screamed.

Wasn't that amazing!

It took me 42 years to come to terms with that traumatic moment! Yes, I forgave them. The process of journaling allowed me to express my emotions. I reflected on the incident and understood why the situation came about. Without his "magic trick," I may still be clinging to my pacifier today! Putting this story into writing, I also allowed my three-year-old self to heal. I've repeated this process for various ages of my inner child.

It has aided me to understand and release pain, sorrow, guilt, and other emotions that burden me. They now exist as mere memories of a near-non-existent version of myself. One that I don't recognise as I am today.

Writing to everyone from my past took eighteen months. I added one final letter to the journal addressed to Archangel Sandalphon. He receives our messages and conveys them to the appropriate guides. In return, they can release you of your karma, offering understanding in many forms in their place. I conducted my first fire-burning ceremony on New Year's Eve at 9 p.m. and burned the journal and the letter. The experience was therapeutic and quite liberating.

Please do consider journaling. It can have a profound and transformative impact on you. Reflect on these memories and express the emotions tied to those past moments. Recognising any pain or hurt your inner child may have felt is essential. This acknowledgement enables you the freedom to express your feelings.

Starting the writing process might feel challenging. Preparing the setting allows you to concentrate and contemplate without distractions. Consider engaging in a guided meditation or light a calming lavender candle. Afterwards, you can listen to relaxing music or do deep breathing exercises. You can kickstart it with an open-ended, intuitive prompt to encourage free-flowing expression. For instance, you could ask, "If I could speak to my younger self right now, what would I say?" This method can bring back memories or emotions your inner child wants to express. Or why not attempt this simple visualisation exercise before you begin writing?

- Close your eyes and picture your younger self in a secure, comfortable environment. Depict the surroundings, sensations, or interactions during that period. Let your intuition lead the way in creating the imagery in your mind's eye.

Now, prepare to write a letter to your inner child. Tap into your empathy to discern what they need to hear. Consider words that convey validation, comfort, and nurturing. Add words of reassurance, support, and encouragement to help you both understand. Trust that everything will be all right.

It is now the moment to envision your inner child responding to your letter. Trust your intuition as you channel the perspective of your younger self. Fusing visualisation into your words, you can uncover even deeper insights. Your inner child will reveal their needs and desires. You can release self-blame or resentment as you empathise with your younger self. It's time to step onto the path of emotional healing.

Completing your letter, write a positive statement that fulfils your inner child's needs. End your writing session by giving thanks for this vital step in the healing process. You've demonstrated your commitment to nurturing your inner child. Make a promise to continue this practice. It will help you heal and gain a new understanding of your life. It's optional to adhere to this practice. The goal is to create self-awareness through compassionate healing.

Always grant your intuition the freedom to guide you. Approach this process with empathy and tenderness. These practices will foster a profound connection with your inner child in time. It's essential to be aware if this part of your healing journey becomes too much. If so, consider seeking extra help from a qualified therapist or counsellor. Your journey of personal growth can begin by answering the following questions.

Do you have any old feelings or experiences you want to deal with by writing in a journal or letters?

How can you ensure you feel safe and supported while going through this?

Are you scared to talk about your feelings or thoughts because of what others might think?

What questions can you use to encourage free expression when writing to your inner child?

Are there any bad feelings or regrets from the past that you can let go of using empathy and inner child healing?

Can you visualise your younger self in a safe and loving space whilst you begin your healing process?

Can you come up with a positive statement to replace negative thoughts?

You need to understand that experiencing empathy for others can enhance your relationships. You will feel vulnerable when you share your thoughts and experiences with others. Yet, in doing so, you encourage them to open up, too. Building trusting relationships will take time and a lot of effort, so be patient. It will need you to use an empathic and intuitive approach. As time passes, your authenticity will shine through in your interactions with others. When in the company of others, be present. Minimise distractions, particularly with your mobile phone. Elevate your intuitive senses by giving each other your undivided attention.

Another poignant time was from my first live Reiki session in 2022. I intended to share healing energy with the world. I saw a surge in my followers from 700 to over 2,000 within six months. Not long afterwards, I revealed to them their comments' impact on me. I shared a photo capturing the moment tears welled in my eyes as I absorbed their pain. I transmuted this pain into unconditional love thanks to Archangel Uriel's brooch. I channel this transformed energy to wherever it is most needed.

Engage in listening, not only to the spoken word but also to what isn't. Observe tone, body language, facial expressions, and gestures to understand someone's life. You want to help by understanding what they are experiencing. You can further explore your understanding of the other person's perspective. Do be mindful of the emotional energy you are investing in. You can confirm their feelings by saying, "I understand why you feel that way. It seems like you're going through a difficult time" demonstrates you are in tune with their emotions.

Gathering more information can reveal emotions your rational mind might have overlooked. It may seem uncomfortable at first. Yet, you can encourage them to open up. Ask open-ended questions which will invite them to share their thoughts and feelings. To stay balanced, trust your gut feelings and understand others' emotions. It will help you see things much more straightforward. Soon, you'll understand others' feelings by putting yourself in their shoes.

Forgiveness is a precious gift you give to yourself. Holding onto anger and resentment harms you more than anyone else. Examine past grievances that are easier to manage.

Observe your thoughts and emotions without judgment so you can establish healthy boundaries. Forgive; it's essential not to hold onto resentment, anger, or pain. You can unravel the path to forgiveness, which applies to you and others. It does not mean you must reconcile with the person who hurt you. Or even condone their actions. It liberates you from resentment and helps you set healthier boundaries.

Treat yourself with kindness and understanding. You're acknowledging that it is OK to feel hurt. Limiting contact with negative individuals can benefit everyone in all cases. You're also admitting that it is also OK to allow yourself to heal. You are detaching from intense emotions linked to injustice. It creates a healthy mental space for healing. Letting go of past grievances can liberate your emotional and mental well-being.

Consider engaging in the following self-care practices to further aid in this journey. They will assist you in shifting your attention to the good things happening right now.

- To practice meditation, focus on the present moment and accept thoughts and feelings.

- Write a letter to the person who hurt you. Use it to express your needs and feelings. Let them know how the situation escalated. The purpose is to release pent-up emotions, not make others aware of further conflict. Burn the letter and bury the ashes afterwards to release negative energy.

- Visualisation: focus on the situation. Visualise the burden lifting off your shoulders, giving you a sense of relief. It can empower you to stay present.

Combining empathy and intuition makes you understand, respect, and care about others. These connections help you understand challenges better. You can then learn to overcome them and succeed. To shed more light on validating your experiences, address the following questions.

Do you ever feel exposed when you share your deepest thoughts and emotions with someone? How did it affect your relationship with that person?

How can you listen in a conversation? What nonverbal cues help you understand others' perspectives?

Can you recall an example of a time when someone validated your feelings? Did it make you feel understood and supported?

How do you practice forgiveness in your life, both for yourself and others? How has it benefited your emotional well-being?

What activities make you happy? How do you practice gratitude for a positive outlook?

What is your understanding of self-forgiveness? How has it changed your life or the lives of those around you?

Cultivating a Love-Centred Mindset

To develop a loving mindset, do things that make life feel fulfilling and meaningful. At the heart of this life-changing journey is cultivating self-love. It would be best if you practised being kind and compassionate to yourself. Focusing on your positive qualities helps rebuild your self-confidence and self-esteem. When you focus on caring for your body, mind, and emotions, it's easier to love yourself. It helps us stay strong and positive when dealing with life's challenges.

Releasing grudges and embracing forgiveness emerges as a liberating gesture of self-compassion. Holding onto negative emotions burdens your emotional well-being. Forgiveness is a transformative step toward personal freedom, even without an apology. This process lets you let go of resentment and feel lighter and more peaceful inside.

Spending time with positive people is essential to avoid feeling less critical. Being around positive people helps you develop a loving mindset. These connections inspire positivity, encouraging the embracement of love, empathy, and compassion. You can handle life's challenges better when you are open-hearted and understanding.

It's vital to set limits and be kind and understanding to handle your emotions. Setting boundaries helps others treat you with the respect and consideration you deserve. These safeguards prevent you from feeling used and promote healthy, respectful relationships.

Engaging in random acts of kindness is a powerful practice. It impacts your mindset and influences others. We can extend our service by holding the door for a stranger or volunteering for a cause. Make someone's day better and inspire a loving mindset. Show kindness and understanding every day.

Recognise that transformation toward a love-centred mindset is gradual. Your patience is a precious gift. Change requires time to develop and strengthen your commitment. Seeking knowledge and insight through books, workshops, and supportive groups is crucial. These resources offer valuable guidance. You can tell your stories to people who have not felt unconditional love.

Embarking on the journey toward a love-centred mindset involves thoughtful practices and experiences. Reflecting on this path, consider how it shapes daily life. How has it contributed to a more fulfilling existence? The methods outlined offer help in this transformative journey. It is not about achieving perfection but embracing life with love. The empathy and compassion directed towards yourself and others. This journey is a lifelong exploration of self-discovery. It will always draw you nearer to embodying a more empathic and loving existence.

What can you do every day to be kind and compassionate to yourself?

Do you recall a situation where you've held onto grudges or resentment? How did this impact your emotional and mental well-being?

Who are the individuals in your life that uplift and inspire you? How does their presence and support contribute to your love-centred mindset?

Think about when you encountered a situation where people were disrespectful to you. How did this situation impact your emotional state? What steps did you take to establish and maintain healthy boundaries?

When did you perform a random act of kindness for someone else? How did this impact both the recipient and you?

How can you practice patience on your journey towards a love-centred mindset?

How do you see your life and attitude changing as you embrace love, empathy, and compassion daily?

Overcoming Fear and Hatred with Unconditional Love

The essence of love, interwoven with intuition and empathy, embodies profound meaning. Explore the transformative potential of unconditional love. It's a force capable of overcoming fear and hatred. This understanding emphasises that unrestrained passion can heal emotional wounds. It fosters compassion and triggers positive transformations within individuals and societies. Emotional healing encourages empathic connections. A new world is about to reveal a path to you. Understanding, acceptance, and harmony mark it.

In an intuitive and empathic sense, unconditional love surpasses boundaries, judgments, and expectations. Flowing from the heart, unburdened by conditions, it embraces others without hesitation. Profound love is pure and selfless. It uplifts and nurtures, connecting individuals beyond present circumstances. It breaks barriers that we can't see, created by our thoughts, and allows us to approach things with more love. It reminds us of the boundless beauty in the human heart - the capacity to offer and receive love.

Confronting hatred, resentment, misunderstandings, and historical wounds, unconditional love champions empathy. It encourages forgiveness through understanding and promotes the acknowledgement of emotional vulnerabilities. It fosters personal growth and positive relationship change. Unconditional love rises above conflict and signs a commitment to moving forward.

Conquering fears often triggers unfavourable behaviours and intolerance. Unconditional love provides a secure space to confront fears. With it, you'll recognise vulnerabilities and discover resilience. To develop as an individual, you need to feel safe, question your views on love, and embrace tolerance.

On a larger scale, unconditional love can inspire collective empathy. Cooperation dismantles prejudice. Valuing shared human experiences fosters dialogue and collaboration. It promotes mutual respect and understanding across diverse backgrounds and beliefs. The partnership of shared objectives addresses social and environmental concerns to combat discrimination.

I was at a local football ground, inviting "The Musketeers" for a New Business Award Nomination. They are my supportive women's networking group. We've accomplished a lot in various fields, and our motto is "One for all and all for one".

This belief shows our support for working together towards progress. Each member shares their knowledge, consenting to the collective advancement of the group. It reflects a collaborative effort. We share our expertise, demonstrating a mutual agreement to progress together.

One of The Musketeers supported a different local football club, which was a rival to the club we were going to. Asking her to attend posed a significant request. It challenged her values and allegiance to her beloved club. Recognising the potential significance of her presence, I engaged in a personal conversation. She hesitated at first but then attended the event as promised. I appreciate her support. It was difficult for her to stop being loyal and join a group of inspiring women. It was an honour having her there, along with the rest of the Musketeers.

Despite tremendous nerves, I didn't win the award, which was disappointing. The next day, I had some moments of introspection with Luci. I realised I had achieved something unique. I found the revelation enlightening when I asked Luci why they nominated me. My mission was terrific and very different to what I was entering. Theirs was to promote equality and gender diversity in male-dominated fields.

Reflection is a valuable tool for understanding

The awards I received were not for personal recognition in my chosen field. The Universe was appreciative of me going above and beyond expectations. The value in it was irrespective of rooted values.

The two popular football teams set aside their rivalry and anger for one evening. This rivalry, spanning generations, showcased our ability to transcend differences. They united in community spirit, regardless of team loyalty. My finalist nomination became an effort to connect people. It emphasised the need to support each other on the path to success in life. It did.

Develop a Deeper Understanding of the Different Forms of Love

Love is a deep and complicated feeling that comes in different forms and ways. It is a significant part of being human. Exploring various aspects of love helps us understand how people connect in relationships. You come across many different virtues which make human emotions unique and intricate. These diverse forms of love infuse our shared journey with depth and meaning.

Romantic love, called Eros, comes from the Greek God of love. It's about being genuine and close in romantic relationships. It combines physical attraction, strong desire, and a deep emotional connection. This form of love carries a yearning for intimate sensuality. Within its embrace, romantic love can ignite a fiery passion. It results in a profound dance of love shared between two individuals.

Another intense, often short-lived form of romantic love is infatuation or crushes. It is most prevalent among teenagers and young adults. This type includes the stronger emotions of love. The attraction and admiration lead to a short-lived feeling of extreme happiness. Romantic love lasts because there is more than superficial interest. It's mature and deep. Adults may also experience infatuation at various junctures in their lives.

Familial love, or Storge, embodies the nurturing connection within the family unit. It encapsulates the bonds shared among parents, children, siblings, and extended family members. Storge's love exhibits a deep sense of responsibility. The unwavering loyalty and compassionate nature functions as a pillar of support. This form of love encompasses self-sacrifice. The individual's protective nature makes them prioritise the well-being of their loved ones.

Platonic love is also known as Philia. It surpasses the confines of ordinary friendship. It ascends to profound levels, rivalling romantic and familial love. This unique bond extends beyond conventional companionship, offering steadfast support and unwavering stability. Platonic love is a strong bond from trust, respect, and shared interests. These cherished relationships are a foundation of shared experiences. It is forging a deep understanding of each other's aspirations, desires, and vulnerabilities.

Love is not for individuals - it includes all living beings and the Earth's ecosystems. It promotes empathy for humanity and the intricate web of the planet's natural world. Universal love comes from the higher realms and connects with Divine love. The love you feel influences how you think and act, helping you understand the Universe more.

Finally, self-love embodies a nurturing self-perception that embraces self-acceptance, self-care, and self-compassion. Treating yourself with kindness, forgiveness, and an awareness of self-worth fulfils emotional needs. Self-love is the base for better relationships, making them more fulfilling and healthy. This love is inspirational to others to prioritise their happiness and needs.

Understanding how people express love can improve relationships and emotional well-being. To better understand passion and the human experience, appreciate its many sides. Love is a unique journey that can shape and enhance your life.

Reflect on your personal experiences of various types of love. Please answer the following questions. They allow you to understand the depth and beauty that love adds to your life. You can appreciate love's impact on relationships and personal growth.

How would you describe the role of romantic love (Eros) in your life? Have you ever felt passion and a deep emotional connection in specific moments?

Have you ever experienced infatuation or crushes? How would you characterise the nature of these feelings in your own life? Do you agree that it can be a temporary state of euphoria?

Do you ever feel responsible and loyal to your family? Do you have compassion for them?

How does Platonic love (Philia) manifest in your friendships? Can you think of times when connections provided support and stability beyond friendship?

Consider your perspective on Universal love. In what ways do you feel connected to all living beings and the Earth's ecosystems? Can you identify moments where you've experienced empathy for the natural world? What changes can you make to help?

How do you practice nurturing self-perception, self-acceptance, and self-compassion daily? Did you ever notice how loving yourself can improve your relationships? Has it inspired others to care for themselves?

Do you find that understanding how people express love helps with complicated relationships? Have you had an experience that made you know people better?

In your opinion, how has love shaped and enhanced your life in profound ways? Have you ever felt fulfilled and transformed by love?

Building trust is crucial for both friendships and romantic partnerships. Examine your feelings in certain situations or around specific individuals. Understand your weaknesses, triggers, and behavioural patterns to aid mindfulness. Being self-aware gives you the confidence to trust your intuition for relationship insights. You always have the freedom to choose who you welcome into your life. They must match your values and needs while also taking into account the feelings of others.

Do embrace this journey of self-trust and trust in others. Honest and open communication is essential in any relationship. You must strive to be there for each other and display reliability. It can encourage others to reciprocate emotional connections whilst respecting personal boundaries. Creating a calm atmosphere helps people feel safe sharing their thoughts and emotions.

Vulnerability requires being open and genuine. You're revealing your fears, insecurities, and emotions. It would be best to acknowledge that everyone also makes mistakes. You'll both need to remain non-judgmental to maintain trust in your relationship. Learn to forgive and extend compassion to each other to heal your relationship. It can deepen your relationships in ways words alone could never achieve. If you hold grudges or resentments, rebuilding trust takes longer and more effort. By contributing, you help build a world of trust and understanding. It leads to new connections and a more united and peaceful world.

So, take a deep breath and allow your heart to open as you respect this journey. All good things take time to unfold. Engaging in heartfelt conversations nurtures loving relationships rooted in empathy and mutual understanding. Let's embark on a transformative journey of visualisation!

Relationships are a remarkable opportunity to explore the depths of your innermost imagination! Envisage these relationships as tending to the roots of a tree! Your expectations of these relationships allow the trunk to stretch skyward and beyond! They form strength and support for everyone you have bonded with. The forces of your intuition and empathy can nourish the deep roots. To encourage their growth, you must go beyond the boundaries of the ordinary. Now, let's explore this imaginary perspective even more.

Imagine yourself at the heart of a vibrant garden encircled by many relationships. Everyone has a unique trait, much like various diverse, colourful plants. These relationships overflow with shared experiences and contagious joy. All are coming together to form a beautiful web of connections. At the centre of this garden, you observe the luscious, fertile soil serving as a symbol of trust. Within it includes the trust you build within yourself. It is a nurturing foundation that allows these relationships to flourish.

Now, consider yourself as a solid and sturdy tree. The branches offer shade and shelter to those around you. As you embody trust, you serve as a sanctuary where people discover solace and a sense of security. Imagine your insights as a clear, winding path. They direct you to each profound connection. As you tread this path, you can feel the authenticity and depth of these bonds. These are the reflections of the unconditional love that flows throughout the garden. Immerse yourself in its warmth, vitality, and splendour. They are all nurtured in the fertile soil of trust and the strength of the protective tree.

Finally, picture your empathy as a gentle rain shower. As it nurtures the garden, recognise the significance. It helps to understand and accept other people's perspectives. Like rain nourishing a garden, empathy fulfils emotional needs in relationships. You are cultivating a sense of closeness and solidarity.

In the grand scheme of your visualisation, it allows you to step into another person's shoes. They share their feelings and understand and respect each other to build a strong bond. You can improve these relationships by thinking and feeling. You have both weathered storms of minor disagreements and heated feuds. The visualisation acts like a soothing balm to heal these wounds. It helps reinforce your inner strength and reminds you of your resilience. You can begin to set healthier boundaries for the future. Stay aware of others' feelings. It works like a magical elixir that restores harmony within your relationships.

Think about these thought-provoking questions before exploring your imagination. They will guide you in delving deeper into the imagery and insights with sincerity and an open mind.

Who are the different plants in your garden symbolising? How did they embody the essence of each relationship?

You are reflecting on the fertile soil of trust at the centre of your garden. How does this trust extend beyond your relationships with others? What role does self-trust play in your visualised sanctuary?

Imagine yourself as the strong tree. How do you feel about providing shade and protection to others? How does this symbolise trust in your awareness?

Do you remember when you felt a strong and genuine connection with someone? What made it stand out as particularly meaningful to you?

Reflect on your visualisation. How might it change the way you nurture and strengthen real-life relationships?

How does empathy's rain shower help you understand how others see things?

What experiences come to mind when stepping into someone else's shoes? Has it deepened your connection or understanding of this relationship?

Balancing Personal and Professional Responsibilities

Balancing personal and professional responsibilities is a common challenge in our fast-paced world. It's crucial to balance your work and personal life to be happy and healthy. Create balance by focusing on tasks and managing your time. You can bring harmony and productivity back into your life.

Discover techniques to decrease stress in your personal and work life. One key system is establishing clear boundaries between your work and personal life. It involves defining specific working hours and adhering to them. Resist the urge to make personal calls at work and not answer emails off the clock.

Mobile phones have made us accessible in today's world, which can lead to assumptions. Being self-employed, people often expect me to be available for spontaneous conversation. Some also expect immediate responses to messages. This expectation persists even during times that are not suitable for work-related matters. Given the ease of constant connectivity, it's natural for these beliefs to arise.

Addressing and managing these expectations is crucial. You need to maintain a healthy balance between your professional and personal life. Open and honest communication is essential in this regard. Set clear boundaries by discussing your availability with friends, family, and clients. Ensure that your time and your work responsibilities are well-defined. This practice helps you find a balance between your personal and work life.

An effective time management tool is the Eisenhower Matrix (or box). People use this tool to decide which tasks are most important. This method helps you focus on work and allows more time for personal activities.

- Urgent and Important (Do First): These tasks need immediate and significant attention. Completing them as soon as possible impacts your goals or well-being.

- Necessary but Not Urgent (Schedule): you must complete these tasks soon to ensure future growth. It allows you to schedule specific times to work on them to prevent them from becoming urgent.

- Urgent but Not Important (Delegate or Limit): these tasks are often time-sensitive and contribute little to your goals. Consider handing off or cutting back on these tasks to free up time for essential duties.

- Not Urgent and Not Important (Minimise or Cut): these tasks are neither essential nor important. They are mere distractions. Scale them down or drop them from your daily routine to maximise productivity.

It can be challenging to balance work and life based on your situation and goals. An essential aspect of finding balance involves recognising your limits. Practise open communication with your employer, colleagues, and family to establish clear boundaries. Discussing ways to solve personal or work problems is crucial to staying balanced. Declining overwhelming tasks and delegating can ease your workload.

To manage your time, include self-care in your daily routine. This method improves your happiness, helps you balance work and life well. Many find balance difficult, but these questions can help you achieve it.

How can you manage your time to care for your well-being and achieve your goals?

How do you manage "Urgent and Important" tasks compared to "Necessary but Not Urgent"? How do you divide your time for each?

How do you separate your personal life from your work life?

Can following set working hours help you balance your personal and professional life? Does minimising personal distractions during work hours contribute to achieving balance?

How does taking breaks and doing things you enjoy help you balance work and life?

How do you prevent distractions from personal messages or work emails when you have time to work?

Have you ever had to give tasks to others or reduce distractions to balance work and life?

What challenges do you face when balancing your personal and professional life? How does it affect communication with your employer, colleagues, and family?

Learning to Trust in Authority Figures

Trusting authority figures means combining intuition with critical thinking in a balanced way. Be aware of your feelings and how you act around authority figures according to your beliefs. This reflective process can be illuminating and informative. Self-reflection will improve your understanding of your reactions. You'll recognise emotional triggers and acknowledge the moments of discomfort around authority.

Be mindful of your emotions when disagreeing with authority figures. They can cloud your usual good judgment. Always strive to maintain emotional composure with rationality. Approach any interactions with an open and transparent mind. It doesn't mean you must surrender your better judgment. You can respond with intuitive understanding and logical reasoning rather than reacting. It can empower you to be more self-aware and confident in your decision. Familiarise yourself with your rights to ensure that your boundaries always remain respected. While open-mindedness is vital, maintaining discernment and critical evaluation is essential. You can then ease improved decision-making with authority figures in any future circumstances.

When assessing an authority figure, look at their qualifications, experience, and past performance. To make a better decision, look into their position and skills. Assess how they match their actions with their words to observe their trustworthiness. Are the steps taken aligned with the responsibility to treat others with respect? If someone's words and actions match, it shows they are trustworthy. This assessment serves as a valuable tool for evaluating their reliability.

Build trust with authority figures with positive interactions and setting clear boundaries. Use proactive communication through questions and seek clarification when needed. Open dialogue demonstrates your commitment to understanding and forging a trustworthy relationship.

Over time, you'll determine if authority figures are trustworthy. With discernment, you can develop resilience and a sense of reliability. Trusting authority figures is not a leap into the unknown. It's a blend of intuition, empathy, and rational thinking. Answer these questions to understand and gain the trust of authority figures.

How do your beliefs influence your actions around authority figures?

Has your beliefs ever affected how you behaved around someone in charge? How has self-reflection helped you understand your reactions to authority figures?

How can you set clear boundaries when interacting with authority figures?

Can you find signs that show whether you can trust someone in charge?

How do you assess an authority figure's trustworthiness over time?

How do you manage your emotions when disagreeing with authority figures?

Have you ever let your emotions affect how you interacted with authority figures?

How do you stay calm when talking to people in charge?

How can you determine if an authority figure is fulfilling their responsibilities?

How can you make sure you have good relationships with authority figures?

Enhancing Communication Skills

Connect better with people by understanding and feeling what others are going through. Improve your communication. Achieving this requires taking specific steps.

- Focus your complete attention on the speaker and refrain from interrupting.

- Attending to verbal and non-verbal cues shows your commitment to a meaningful conversation.

- Place their perspective above your response to adopt their attentiveness.

- Remain aware of your body language, facial expressions and tone. Your actions can convey enthusiasm or disinterest.

Respond with empathic validation when someone shares their thoughts or emotions with you. Reflect on their words. You're demonstrating attentiveness, encouraging a deeper discussion through open-ended questions. Avoid asking questions with only a "yes" or "no" answer. These questions don't allow for a deep and meaningful conversation. Instead, opt for an open-ended question like, "Could you share more about your thoughts?" By asking these questions, you show understanding and make the conversation more interesting.

Another skill is to refrain from rushing to offer immediate solutions to problems. In my experience, people sometimes seek acknowledgement rather than answers. Before my awakening, I often disagreed with friends due to my impartial stance. I rarely take sides, as I can see different aspects of situations.

I have offered explanations and solutions to discussions and arguments. Unfortunately, some could not see beyond their immediate circumstances. It's about something other than being right, despite my clear perspective. It's about considering the possibilities of gaining a better understanding. Trust your instincts when inquiring about more profound aspects of conversations. The goal is to resolve only some issues through communication. It's also about creating a considerate atmosphere.

It helps others accept solutions when they're ready without the impact of saying, "I told you so".

You'll have the discernment to determine when to offer help and when not to. Listening shows your engagement and helps clear up misconceptions. It doesn't mean you should be a receptacle for people to vent their frustrations. Or for you to absorb any or all their anger. As time passed, I noticed that my friendships started to fade. Because I stood up for myself, I refused to tolerate mistreatment. I could feel their anger, too. Setting healthy boundaries is an absolute must.

You've encountered the quote, "Don't shoot the messenger but...". I've learned that giving them solutions can be beneficial if people are ready. It is particularly relevant when individuals have a distinct purpose or life path. My intervention could either obstruct or drag out the realisation of that purpose. It may set off an unnecessary chain of consequences. In the long run, it affects other situations and individuals. Furthermore, it could lead to more karmic lessons; no one needs to go through that!

Understanding that people express thoughts and feelings to communicate well is essential. People have distinct preferences, sharing ideas in great detail, while others prefer brevity. To connect and establish rapport with others, understand these unique communication styles. Please observe the speaker's signals and respond to their emotions. Being adaptable helps people interact better. It also shows a real commitment to understanding and respecting others. Practice will refine your reactions, making you better at connecting and providing support. Stay aware and use these techniques to be a compassionate and successful communicator.

Building Trust in Others and Expressing Opinions

You can forge a new path in a life that resonates with your principles. Developing self-awareness builds a strong belief in your authenticity and boosts confidence. Reflecting and examining particular views and opinions can hold great significance.

Building rapport makes it easy for people to share opinions in an open environment. Be mindful that not everyone will share your views. It's essential always to respect the diversity of thought. Listening to your gut feeling can help you know when and where to have meaningful talks. Establishing an environment of trust creates a platform of transparency for equality. Remain authentic by engaging in open dialogue. Avoid pretending to agree to avoid conflict. Others will then express their thoughts and emotions without fearing criticism.

Remember, you can clarify your instincts through careful observation. Being attentive to words, tone, and body language shows respect for another's viewpoints. If you are open to feedback, it shows you are open to discussion with others. Listen without reacting with a negative or positive response. If you doubt something, recognise your feelings to prevent biases from influencing you. It sharpens your intuitive awareness to identify reciprocal behaviour with constructive interactions. When people get along and are genuine, it sparks creative and inspiring problem-solving. These conversations highlight areas for improvement to encourage growth through learning.

It's essential to remain diplomatic in personal and professional situations. The following questions aim to build trust with others. You can share your thoughts in ways that nurture positive connections.

How can you listen to others and show that you value their perspective?

What non-verbal cues can you use to convey openness and trustworthiness in conversations?

How can you show genuine interest in others' perspectives before sharing your opinions?

How does empathy contribute to establishing trust when expressing your opinions?

How can you handle disagreements and conflicts to maintain trust and respect?

How can you express your opinions while also being open to different viewpoints?

How can you provide constructive feedback without being critical or argumentative?

To live a fulfilling life, you must embrace love and have a positive mindset. You exhibit behaviours that nurture love, kindness, and compassion in all situations. To make every interaction meaningful, include love and stay in the present moment. It involves prioritising understanding over judgment. Choose empathy and forgiveness over indifference and resentment. You're creating a harmonious and compassionate existence. It will attract enriching relationships and experiences to your life.

To embark on this journey:

• Start by nurturing self-love and self-compassion. Extend kindness and care to yourself as you would to others.

• Seek to comprehend the perspectives and emotions of those around you. Practise active listening and empathising with their experiences.

• Practice mindfulness exercises to stay present. You are to be able to respond to situations with love and compassion.

Recognise the good things in your life. The people with you on this journey can help you love yourself more. When faced with challenging situations, focus on deep listening without interruptions. You can show empathy by nodding, making eye contact, and using understanding phrases. If emotions escalate, consider taking a break to cool off. You can revisit the discussion at a more conducive time.

Express gratitude for the support of those around you. You're fostering shared connections with cherished individuals. Establishing healthy boundaries safeguards dignity and prevents exploitation when sharing sensitive information. Equip yourself with conflict resolution skills that prioritise love and empathy. Frame concerns that centre on feelings and needs rather than blaming others. Breathing and avoiding raised voices contribute to maintaining emotional balance during heavy discussions. Sincere apologies can aid in conflict resolution. In some cases, involving a neutral third party can help open communication.

Forgiveness becomes a potent means to move beyond conflicts. You're liberating yourself from unnecessary emotional baggage.

Also, avoid trying to win arguments. Instead, align your thoughts, actions, and behaviours to find solutions. Patience with others is crucial to enhancing decision-making and cultivating a serene life. It encourages composure and understanding, especially in adversity or awaiting desired outcomes.

Remaining open to receiving love in its various forms is essential. If you trust the Universe, it will bring loving relationships that match your destiny. It leads to patience and growth. Demonstrating love, kindness, and compassion sets an example to others. You're helping people connect better, be happier, and create a more loving world. So, on behalf of the Universe, thank you for fostering love and positivity.

Cultivating Healthy and Empowering Relationships

Connections give people power in different relationships, like friendships, romance, family, and work. To cultivate meaningful interactions, rely on tools of intuition and empathy. When we fear judgment or ridicule, speaking up can enhance understanding. You're listening to foster a reciprocal exchange. This process can help you make real connections and feel heard and valued. It creates a supportive environment based on trust.

Empowering relationships thrive on intuition. They encourage growth and identify hopes and dreams. They unlock secrets as you support each other in tough times. You're validating feelings and creating a judgment-free environment, leading to mutual empowerment. It is important to value each other's perspectives in relationships. Recognising imperfections and setting healthy boundaries is crucial. Open and equal communication fosters equality and shared responsibility. This approach resolves differing opinions while preserving separate identities.

Creating supportive and nurturing environments allows both parties to reach their full potential. It stresses the importance of a genuine desire to connect with others and the world. Taking mutual pride in each other's achievements emphasises the importance of personal space. In summary, empowering relationships contribute to all individuals' emotional development.

The following questions highlight the importance of mutual goals, respect, and responsibility. Allow them to guide you towards a more satisfying and purposeful life. Your responses can help you apply these principles within your relationships.

How do your relationships affect your emotional well-being and personal growth?

How can your intuition and empathy contribute to fostering and empowering your relationships?

How does understanding how others feel and what they worry about help build trust?

How can valuing others' opinions improve your relationships?

How does supporting each other's goals help you grow in your relationships?

Why is it important to handle conflicts and disagreements in your relationships?

How can relationship empowerment affect the well-being and personal development of all individuals?

Building Confidence in Social Interactions

Intuition and empathy are essential in personal and professional interactions. They become potent tools, weaving the fabric of genuine connections with unwavering confidence. These qualities will influence your journey. Have you ever liked or disliked someone when you first met them? That is your intuition in action. It is down to you to assess and establish the elusive clues hidden behind the unspoken words.

As you practise active listening, you mirror and reflect on the message received. It shows your genuine comprehension and helps build trust. Improving your intuition and empathy makes it easier to understand hidden meanings. Your skill in interpreting non-verbal cues simplifies handling new conversations. It also helps you exit challenging ones too. You're assisting others to move beyond surface-level interactions. You create a safe place to share genuine thoughts and support others. It allows them to let go of initial judgments and preconceived notions. Working together, you help steer conversations to provide a broader emotional perspective.

At this point, it's a good idea to think back and remember essential talks with others. Engaging in transparent and genuine conversations is a fundamental aspect of personal growth. Think about how these traits have affected your interactions. This practice can heighten your awareness for intuitive insights for future conversations. Remember, you can attempt role reversal.

The ability to approach diverse social interactions enables you to connect with others. Enriching your relationships gives you the confidence to engage in every interaction. Practising these skills, a complicated web of connections becomes a rewarding journey. You're working with others to build meaningful relationships in a new world. Take some time with this in mind to consider the following questions. Your responses can enrich your knowledge for cultivating confidence in many social interactions.

Have you ever connected with someone on a deep level when you first met them? Did it leave a lasting impact on your relationship?

What methods do you adopt when engaging in active listening? How do these practices enhance trust within your relationships?

Can you remember when your gut feeling helped you find hidden feelings while talking? How did this awareness impact your response?

How can you adopt their perspective to empathise with someone else?

How can you get a better understanding and express emotions in social situations?

Connecting with Past Life Origin and Purpose

Exploring your past life origin and purpose can be an enriching discovery. Although many individuals believe in reincarnation, many do not. I have encountered many past-life removals in my energy healing practice. None of them are as dramatic as the exorcisms in movies! These energies have originated from the highest importance to the humblest of backgrounds. Each one presents a reason to still be on Earth.

In most cases, they have been emotional and desperate to return home. Others embrace their fate, influenced by their experiences on Earth. Either way, you must approach this investigation with sincere curiosity. Here are some ways to use intuition and empathy to connect with your past life origin and purpose.

Many regression practitioners help people explore their past lives and move forward. These trained therapists allow you access to past moments affecting you in this life. Regression therapy can help with many emotional and psychological problems. It is a valuable tool for exploring and addressing these issues. If you're interested, find a trustworthy regression therapist to help you.

You can use guided meditations to access your subconscious mind. They help you imagine going back in time or to a different place. Before starting, establish the intention for insight that assists you in the present. Begin by quieting your mind and focus on your breathing. As you relax, use your empathy to imagine yourself in a different time, culture, or situation. Join this activity and trust your gut to grasp the emotions and experiences.

Writing with intuition can reveal your purpose from a past life in a therapeutic manner. The writer allows their intuitive thoughts to pour onto the page without overthinking. This tool is valuable for exploring past lives. It doesn't have self-censorship, criticism, or rigid logical order. Grammar doesn't matter.

Doing other creative things, like abstract art, helps you test your gut feelings. You're allowing your hands to guide your expression without rationalising your actions. The creations from your activities could offer glimpses into many past life experiences. As you settle into this exploration, let your mind wander. Pose a question: "What images, places, or historical periods are surfacing in my mind?" See what comes about.

Your creations may have profound insight into the skills that have felt natural to you.

Dream interpretation often involves connecting with the psychological elements of your subconscious thoughts. The feelings from them can transform into memories. Have you had recurring dreams, fears, or interests that could connect with a past life? Analysing your dreams can offer valuable insights into your present psychological state. The responses can add awareness to your emotions and concerns about life circumstances. To begin, have a dream journal nearby and write down any memories as soon as you wake up. If you write down your dreams daily, you might remember essential memories. Use your intuition to decipher symbols or signs suggesting potential past life experiences.

Stay open to meaningful coincidences and gut feelings in your daily life. Keep track of patterns or emotions that connect to specific times or experiences. These could hold significance in shedding light on who you once were.

Exploring yourself with kindness and an open mind in this new way can be challenging. Strive to remain receptive to any insights or emotions that emerge. Keep in mind that the pursuit of your past life origin and purpose is unique to your journey. The revelations will vary, so balance intuition, empathy, and critical thinking. The ultimate goal is to understand who you are and live in the present. Your life purpose and the lessons experienced help you evolve and transform. Regardless of any preexisting beliefs, try to remain open to intuitive suggestions.

Impostor syndrome is a cognitive perception in which individuals struggle with self-doubt. People worry about appearing fake or dishonest, no matter what they achieve. People with impostor syndrome struggle with feeling unworthy of their success. When people believe they have tricked others, signs and emotions show. These can include:

- Overachievement: an individual works extra hard and accomplishes a lot. They feel they must make up for thinking they are not good enough.

- Fear of exposure: an individual is always anxious that someone will find out they are. They need to be more skilled and knowledgeable than they think you are.

- Discounted success: individuals feel uncomfortable receiving credit for their skills or efforts. They believe success is due to luck or help from others.

- Difficulty accepting praise or recognition: individuals find receiving honour or glory hard. It makes them uncomfortable when others acknowledge their achievements.

- Seeking validation is when an individual depends on constant validation to confirm competency.

If you realise you have impostor syndrome, you should reflect and seek support. Impostor syndrome can make people feel inadequate in various parts of their lives. It does not discriminate based on gender, age, or occupation. It can affect those starting on their paths and those already successful. Incorporating any of the following techniques will help cultivate a positive mindset. You can reduce the impact of imposter syndrome to develop a healthier self-perception.

Begin by being more aware of all your accomplishments, skills, and experiences. Recognising, appreciating, and celebrating small victories can be effective. The most minor achievements shift your attention from what you have yet to do. The work you have invested in will have been challenging to reach your current position.

Recognise that you're a work in progress. Believe in your instincts. They remind you of your unique value to others and yourself.

Keep a success journal. Write down what you achieve, compliments, and positive feedback. Review your diary for a significant boost in confidence. It serves as a powerful reminder of your capabilities whenever you need it.

To be self-compassionate, treat yourself kindly and understand yourself as you know others. It reminds us that everyone faces challenges and self-doubt at different times. When you notice self-critical thoughts creeping in, counter them with self-compassionate affirmations. Remind yourself that "I'm doing my best," "I deserve to be here," or "It's okay to make mistakes."

You realise and empathise with others to see that even confident people can feel fake. Understanding their feelings will teach you that you are not alone in this struggle. Engage in conversations; share your experiences. It can go a long way in normalising impostor syndrome and reduce its impact in future situations. If you need help or advice, contact friends, colleagues, or mentors. They can offer constructive input and validation for any concerns you may face. Talk about imposter syndrome to gain different perspectives and understand it better.

Challenging negative thoughts through cognitive reframing has the power to transform your beliefs. When you find yourself thinking that you are not good enough, take a moment to question that belief. Ask yourself for concrete evidence to the contrary. What specific achievements or skills prove your competence? This practice can replace self-doubt with a more realistic perspective. Remind yourself of the enduring strength to achieve past successes.

When you imagine your future success, you feel confident in your abilities. This practice can rewire your brain to enhance your self-assurance. Set realistic expectations and acknowledge that perfection is an unattainable standard. Recognising that everyone makes mistakes can help you gain valuable insight. Instead of seeing mistakes as failures, you can see them as chances to improve. To develop a growth mindset, remember that practising and learning can make you an expert. Participating in professional development can help you enhance your skills and knowledge. It will also help boost your confidence.

As you continue to grow and improve, take breaks to consider why your progress is essential. By looking inward, you can test your methods and embrace a positive attitude. Approach this inner exploration with openness and honesty. Within this process, you may discover more profound insights about yourself. To understand your efforts better, reflecting and gaining valuable insights is helpful. You elevate your self-worth by integrating these techniques to nurture a positive mindset. Building a solid base for personal growth and self-compassion is part of the journey.

How can you practice self-awareness daily to help you address impostor syndrome?

Can you think of a specific accomplishment or skill you are proud of? How does acknowledging and appreciating such achievements enhance your self-esteem?

Can you give an example of when you changed negative thoughts about your abilities?

Which self-compassionate affirmations resonate most with you? How can you incorporate them into your inner dialogue during self-doubt?

Did discussing impostor syndrome with friends, colleagues, or mentors give you new insights?

Can writing your achievements in a journal boost your confidence and reduce self-doubt?

How can envisioning success play a role in overcoming impostor syndrome? Which specific goals or situations would enjoy this practice?

How can you set realistic goals and understand that perfection isn't achievable?

Utilising Energy Healing Meditations for Self-Awareness

Engaging in energy-healing meditations can enhance self-awareness through intuitive and empathic exploration. Reflect by setting clear goals and considering various factors to understand situations better. To create a tranquil atmosphere:

- Make sure to find a space where no one will disturb you.

- Light a candle and play some soothing music designed for meditation.

- Consider using some aromatic essential oils to help you unwind.

- Sit, close your eyes, and take deep, cleansing breaths. Relax your body and release any tension.

Prepare yourself for a meditative body scan by reading the following in advance. Imagine your seven main energy centres, starting at the bottom of your back and moving up to the top of your head. Envision each chakra as a warm, radiant light, spinning with vibrant energy. As you connect, be aware of any sensations, colours, or emotions associated with them. As you encounter challenging feelings or thoughts, allow them to surface without resistance. Visualise them as low energy, ready to transform into unconditional love. Let your thoughts and feelings come in. Trust your inner guidance without judging or analysing. Observe your emotions as they dissipate to make way for healing light. Use your breath to inhale positivity and exhale negativity.

- Root Chakra (base of the spine): visualise a vibrant red light. Explore a recent decision by posing, "Does this choice make me feel safe and secure?"

- Sacral Chakra (lower abdomen): visualise a sparkling orange light. When making a decision, posing, "Does this make me feel creative or sensual?"

- Solar Plexus Chakra (higher abdomen): visualise a bright yellow light. Consider a decision posing, "Does this choice ignite a sense of empowerment within me?"

153

- Heart Chakra (centre of your chest): visualise a soothing green and pink healing light. Expanding throughout your body, feeling this love. "How can I attract more love and empathy into my daily life?"

- Throat Chakra (base of throat): visualise a soothing blue light. To improve communication and express yourself more, ask, "How can I be better?"

- Third Eye Chakra (middle of your brow): visualise an indigo light. Concentrate on trusting your intuition, posing, "How can I improve my awareness? How can I trust in the insights I receive through my intuition?"

- Crown Chakra (top of your head): visualise a radiant violet or white light. To understand your mental imagery, pose, "How can I trust what I see through Divine guidance?"

To conclude your meditation, embrace a positive affirmation tied to your self-awareness. Say out loud, "I trust my intuition," "I am open to valuable insights," or "I am worthy of self-compassion." Offer gratitude for the insights and emotions that surfaced during your practice. Bring back your awareness of your physical surroundings. Move your fingers and toes, take more deep breaths, and open your eyes when ready. Take a moment for reflection before documenting your experience.

Four years ago, I started meditating and dreaming of being on stage. I shared my healing journey and wisdom with others. I talked about trusting your intuition and sending healing energy. I even envisioned inviting an audience member onto the stage. The intention was to share their story on their behalf despite having never met them before. They shared a sad and traumatic experience, releasing the burden of guilt. This hidden purpose added a deeper layer of significance to the occasion.

I have yet to experience my vision as I write this, but I help people release their burdens. Each step brings me closer to achieving this vision.

The true essence lies not in the goal, for your Higher Self already awaits you there and with open arms. It is to unearth the keys that unlock the doors of opportunity within our journey. Do not let your fears hold you back. Take advantage of what you can have right now. There's no need to wait for the future to unfold. You're making it happen right now! Embrace the joy within your reach right now, and trust your purpose. My story serves as a reminder to embrace your journey. Have faith in yourself and keep opening those doors of opportunity as and when they appear to you.

Practising energy healing meditations helps you connect more with your intuition and emotions. You'll foster self-awareness and emotional healing for personal growth.

Understanding your feelings helps you grasp your life purpose and your journey's essence. Take charge of your destiny! Seize the present moment and mould it into the vision you want to cherish. Unlock your full potential and enjoy a satisfying life by committing and planning. Your goals should not be distant dreams. They are destinations waiting for your unwavering efforts to transform them into reality. Prepare yourself and dare to dream! Aim high and let your inner strength guide you. Future success and contentment are yours to embrace. Beat your drum; the Universe can hear you loud and clear!

My story is about discovering myself, listening to my inner guidance, and trusting it. It takes bravery to embrace uncertainty. Despite temporary challenges, instinctive and self-centred choices lead to long-term benefits. Having faith in the unfolding path is commendable! At 45, if someone asked about my future, I couldn't have imagined being 'The Spiritual Engineer'! My progress and hope for a better future show my ability to change and reach goals.

I started my journey as "Ickle Pixie Oracles." I had a picture of me standing next to a shop window. The window had a quote that said, "Something beautiful is happening." I became a Reiki Master but couldn't teach it because of my unique energy-healing work. At that point, I transformed into "The Selenite Sword." It was then I began specialising in releasing karmic attachments for individuals. Finally, beginning a new journey, I adopted the brand "Melissa Grewar - The Spiritual Engineer." It was a moment of full circle when I stood outside the same shop five years later with the exact quote.

Every moment is beautiful

Every moment, thought, and action affects positive life changes, both good and bad. Revisiting past traumas helps to release them, and this transformation has benefited me. It has had a positive impact on others all over the world.

To achieve your goals, you must first define what success means to you. Immerse yourself in a mental picture of your ideal future. Identify the knowledge and skills required to achieve your goals. Invest in learning from mentors who align with your values at each stage of your development. Their experiences can help steer you on your personal development journey. When times are tough, being with supportive people can make you feel better. Your achievements can even be a source of giving back to the community or causes that matter most to you. You inspire others with a deep sense of fulfilment and a greater sense of purpose.

Think about what's most important to you. Recognise what you're good and bad at, foster your interests, and compare them to your plans. Your deep understanding of your past will show you the right direction. By reflecting on yourself, you can understand your true self and make better choices. You're chartering a unique life experience on your terms.

This guide helps you make your dreams come true and stay true to yourself and your values. It serves as a reminder that success is an ongoing adventure, not a final destination. Each step is a chance to grow and find fulfilment. Revisiting your mental and written representations of success helps maintain motivation. It helps to focus on the evolving journey and make necessary changes to the plan. Making efficient decisions and setting realistic deadlines turns your goals into reality. This strong vision will motivate you, turning success from an idea into something you can see.

Setting Realistic and Achievable Goals

Setting achievable goals is essential for your personal and professional growth. When setting goals, follow basic principles that act as a blueprint for your life. Ensuring your objectives are clear and well-defined, focus on short-term and long-term goals. To be successful in life, consider your work, personal growth, relationships, and health. A framework helps you stay motivated and focused on your goals.

Crafting an action plan is crucial when achieving your goals. Divide your big goals into smaller, manageable steps to navigate your path. The SMART Goals approach offers clarity and direction. It can include a timeline that matches your ability to achieve the desired outcome. There are other ways to set realistic and attainable objectives besides SMART Goals. Adopt a disciplined approach that suits your needs and allows you to start setting goals. You can manage your time and resources to leave space for other activities.

The WOOP method sets goals by focusing on wishes, outcomes, obstacles, and plans. Start by stating your "Wish" and identify what you want to achieve. To increase your chances of reaching your "Outcome", imagine the good results and how they will impact you. Recognise potential "Obstacles" or challenges that could get in your way. Make a simple "Plan" that shows the steps and strategies to overcome obstacles and reach your goal. This method offers a simple and practical roadmap to turn your dreams into reality.

Try approaching your goals in a different way with Backward Goal Setting. Instead of immediate tasks, begin with your long-term vision or ultimate goal. Work backwards to create milestones and specific actions leading to your destination. This method builds a smooth connection between your long-term and short-term goals. It allows you to progress toward achieving your overarching vision.

A creative approach to goal setting is through Narrative Goal Setting. It turns your goals into a compelling story about your future self. I use this method for intuitive readings and share them on social media. Viewing life as a fairy tale with a happy ending can make life more enjoyable and impactful. Creating an illustrative account of your journey makes it inspiring. It transforms goal-setting into a fulfilling and motivating journey.

Embracing any of these principles empowers you to create attainable and transformative goals. They will propel you forward on your path of personal and professional development. Goal setting is a dynamic, ongoing process. It will reflect your evolving aspirations and capabilities. It's not about the destination but a journey of personal growth through self-discovery. As you navigate this journey, re-evaluate and redefine your goals as needed. Please keep them in alignment with your changing circumstances and newfound insights. Being flexible helps you stay motivated. It also keeps your goals aligned with who you're becoming.

Integrating Learned Skills into Everyday Life

It's essential to use your skills in your everyday life for personal growth. Developing your skills can inspire you. The benefits are achieving goals, feeling satisfied, and getting more career chances. These skills are the foundation for progress. They allow you to face challenges and adapt to changes. They give you the power to expand your horizons, try new things, and improve your life.

A well-defined action plan is essential to incorporate these skills into your life. As you improve your intuition, this method gives you purpose, motivation, and self-trust. A clear plan to improve music, language, and personal development skills is essential. This plan will guide your natural growth and empathy. You can stay focused on your journey of change. It acts as your compass, showing your efforts in alignment with your soul's desires.

To improve your intuition, focus on developing specific skills and directing your energy. Please only try to help some people with their problems and requests. Concentrated time and energy are vital for crafting your master plan. You can set aside time for practising your intuition in your daily routine. If you develop this mindset in your everyday life, it will help you achieve your goals. This adaptable approach becomes your most influential tool. You can reflect on past achievements to navigate challenges.

Stay on track to improve your skills. It's essential to assess your progress and make adjustments. Overcoming challenges and obstacles is part of learning. Trusting your intuition helps you overcome them. Seeking feedback is valuable in advancing your intuitive development. Feedback that enables you to improve and refine your skills can speed up your progress. Embrace feedback as a tool for personal growth rather than criticism.

Use your intuition at work, hobbies, and daily tasks to find opportunities. Practice is the key to your mastery. Stay informed about your ongoing progress is crucial for sustaining your expertise. Avoid unnecessary involvement in other people's conflicts. It seldom benefits you and may only serve as another reminder to trust your intuition.

Tracking your progress is a tool in project management that helps document evidence. These tools help you see all your tasks and work well with others. It will give you the support and motivation to finish them. Sharing a problem with someone often makes it easier to handle. Please simplify your workflow to improve your time management efficiency.

To remember everything:

- Write essential tasks, events, and deadlines on a calendar

- Create a list that offers a clear plan for task completion

- Break down goals into manageable steps you can check off as you do them

It helps you get more done and stay focused on reaching your goals. Recognise and celebrate achievements, especially with those who have helped you. It can inspire you to improve your intuitive abilities. As time passes, you will see the good changes you have made that enhanced your life in different ways.

A significant occasion occurred when I enrolled on some spiritual workshops. I felt let down when I could not secure a spot in the year-long course that evolved from them. I was unaware of the Universe's alternate intentions for my journey. A few months later, I enrolled on a yearlong Angelic course. Again, this propelled me to another state of enlightenment. This decision I have not regretted and one that has enriched my path.

I learned a valuable lesson: education is about acquiring all knowledge. Including the basics, learning should be about knowing what's essential for your job. Excessive deadlines influence our perception of time, unlike the eternal Universal time. We chastise ourselves for missing deadlines and believe we have missed the opportunity. It is wise to plan for the future, but living in the present is essential. Discovering your purpose helps you guide yourself and assist others in finding theirs. Embrace change. It opens doors for opportunities to help you achieve your goals for catalyst growth.

Planning for Long-Term Growth and Success

Achieving long-term success involves open-minded personal development, purposeful thinking, and goal setting. You can achieve your life goals by developing trust in yourself and others. Remember that this journey is ongoing and may unfold more than anticipated.

To embark on this path, you need to explore the available opportunities. Begin by creating a plan for both short-term and long-term growth and success. Prepare by identifying what you must let go of to create space for what you wish to receive. Identify obstacles to plan solutions. You can break them into manageable steps to stay focused and motivated.

To ensure organisation, create a timeline for each phase of your plan. To stay focused on completing tasks, include a timeframe for each step in your schedule. You can adjust this timeline to ensure progress towards your goals.

Here are some examples that show how to plan for long-term success in your life.

- To achieve your goal of embracing new opportunities, you need to be open to positive changes. Your plan will include accepting short-term opportunities that present themselves. These may lead you toward your desired destination. Try to maintain a positive and focused mindset. Change can be overwhelming if you're unsure or stepping out of your comfort zone. It paves the way for new possibilities and personal growth through diverse experiences.

- If you want to move, make a plan. Find information about the new place, find a place to live, look for work, and get to know the community. Flexibility and organisation are essential in this endeavour. Don't hesitate to seek help when needed. Relocating can be an exhilarating yet daunting adventure. Take the time to explore and establish connections before making life-altering decisions. Reversals may not always be possible.

- If your goal entails distancing yourself from negative influences, include establishing healthy boundaries. Communicate your needs by seeking support from friends and family. Releasing relationships that no longer serve you prioritises your well-being and happiness.

163

- To welcome someone, your plan should involve building trust. Allow yourself to be vulnerable and show appreciation for others' contributions. To communicate well, find ways to include them in your daily routine. Be willing to listen and learn from each other. It can be a rewarding experience. Cherish the journey of nurturing this relationship into reality.

- Suppose you want to find a new job without your current employer knowing. Aim to maintain professionalism and discretion throughout the process. Update your CV and cover letter before researching employers. Schedule interviews outside work hours. It's essential to refrain from discussing it with coworkers or clients.

When planning for your success, it's essential to trust your instincts and do what feels right. Every situation is unique, so take time to reflect on your goals and values to create a plan in alignment with them. Trust your intuition when making decisions about your goals. It will guide you and prevent mistakes. Make your well-being and happiness a priority. Be bold and ask for help from reliable people. Sometimes, you may encounter unexpected changes or difficulties. These may be more beneficial for your long-term plans than your short-term objectives.

Stay flexible and remain open to these unexpected twists and turns. Remember, you have the courage and trust to believe that the Universe has your back!

Addressing Financial Responsibilities and Money Mindset

If you want to improve your career and money management, there's an easy way. Trust your intuitive feelings. Begin by focusing on creating a roadmap that aligns and evolves with your future vision. This well-balanced approach provides a solid foundation to build your aspirations into reality.

You need to be able to understand how to manage your finances. Learning the basics of monetary management should be a gradual process. When making a financial plan, trust your intuition to help you meet your goals. Show empathy towards your future self to pay off debts and save money. You can take charge by using your knowledge and gut feelings to make a money plan.

To establish a clear goal for what you want to achieve, explore how your earnings can ease this journey. Consider what brings you excitement and happiness. Your financial needs must complement your personal needs. Your intuition will always guide you towards areas where passion and potential live. To remain motivated, you need to stay open-minded. Opportunities will present themselves to allow new insight for skill development. When facing adversity, maintaining your motivation for career advancement is crucial. Mindfulness will help you welcome any mistakes. They're essential tools for becoming the best version of yourself.

Realising how financial stability affects career success is vital to a fulfilling life. Delving deeper involves unpacking the critical components for a solid financial foundation. Managing finances in alignment with your goals can help sustain your passion. Self-reflection also serves as a roadmap for aligning career ambitions with financial stability. Your plan must cover budgeting, savings, investments, and debt management. You can navigate the complex terrain of finance and career to lead you to a more fulfilling life. To help guide you with purpose, answer the following questions.

What are your current career goals, and how do they relate to your financial objectives?

What is your usual approach to making financial decisions in your life? In what ways could your intuition influence those decisions?

How do you currently manage your finances? Where do you see opportunities for improvement with your career goals?

How can you incorporate your intuition and empathy into your financial decisions?

Can you recall when following your intuition led to a positive financial outcome? What did you learn from that experience?

How can you balance pursuing your career goals with managing your finances?

How can you stay motivated when you face challenges in your career journey?

Intuition can be an early warning for sudden career or workplace changes. To understand different perspectives, consider the impact of your choices on others. Listen to their opinions. It can help you determine the best time to approach, discuss, and solve upcoming conflicts. As you adapt more to changes, you can assist those struggling. Understanding their perspective through active listening uncovers their unspoken needs. These pain points often signify unmet desires. Everyone can now enjoy innovative ideas for creative solutions.

My success has taken different forms, often unfolding along a winding, obstacle-laden road. You can still reach your destination and learn something along the way. Embrace the uniqueness of this journey and particularly the lessons you must overcome. Try to avoid fixating on achieving your goals exactly as your mind envisions.

Throughout my career, I have always followed a challenging path. Over time, this has gained valuable insights. These lessons still act as a guide for me today. I can use this understanding to help others overcome similar experiences. I could have had a better education if I didn't listen to my spiritual mentors. My teachers hadn't observed my visual impairment for some years, either. I also switched schools many times when I was younger, making my academic path more difficult. Much of this served as a purpose for understanding the needs of others.

Over time, I leaned on social impact courses to support my career goals. These pursuits always came with challenges. The goal was to show me where I was going wrong - problems with work, education, money, and instructors. These experiences helped me mature and see the value of "trusting the process". Understanding your past enables you to recognise different paths and opportunities. I know when I am on the right track when the help I need comes without conflict.

Everyone and everything teaches us lessons

I must trust my intuitive and empathic decisions, and so must you. They always lead you to the right opportunities. These opportunities will open doors and guide you to suitable options.

Prioritising everyone's well-being can foster a supportive workplace. It is also essential to balance understanding others' needs and your own. Empathy can enable you to identify when others might be experiencing burnout. You're shaping who you're becoming to contribute to your success. At the same time, you are also using your empathy to understand what you need to excel in these areas. Answering the following questions helps you persevere with your goals. They will guide you to do what feels right.

How can your intuition warn you about changes or challenges in your job or workplace?

How can you use your intuition to know the best time to approach and solve potential conflicts at work?

How can you learn from the perspectives of others when your decisions affect them?

Why is it essential to have a work environment where we help and care for each other?

How can empathy help you recognise signs of burnout in yourself or your colleagues at work?

How can you help people with career problems by being open to change and adapting to new situations?

How can you understand the needs of people changing careers when listening to them?

Did your journey change how much you trust exploring different careers and opportunities?

Has your intuition helped you find the right chances to advance in your career?

Developing Resourcefulness in Problem-Solving

Problem-solving is the art of uncovering solutions to challenges and obstacles. The first step is identifying the issue. Then, we delve into its root cause. Finally, we develop a strategic plan to overcome it. When you establish resourceful thinking, you can face challenges with an open mind. To make decisions, rely on intuition, empathy, and thinking for analysis. Practical problem-solving is a versatile skill applicable to all areas of life. You can explore various perspectives by breaking complex issues into more manageable components. Your future decisions will now rely on the information and resources available.

Mastering the art of finding alternative solutions demands flexibility in your approach. You can tap into your intuitive thinking to navigate through challenges. Most days, you will generate ingenious solutions to overcome initial problems. On other days, you might encounter limitations or other constraints. It requires transcending traditional limits to maximise resources and adapt your strategy. Trust your instincts and intuition, especially when thinking about new ideas.

When you trust your intuition, you allow your creativity to flow. To develop resourcefulness:

- Take a moment to relax

- Contemplate the problem without overthinking it.

- Quiet your mind and let your inner thoughts and ideas surface.

- Refrain from dismissing them, especially if they seem unconventional or far-fetched.

Imaginative ideas can lead to innovative solutions. In time, you'll find that you can uncover hidden opportunities. You can repurpose existing resources to achieve your desired results.

Creative thinking is a vital skill that empowers individuals. The art of unravelling complex challenges is to break them.

To solve problems, be innovative and flexible. Also, consider how others feel about your ideas.

For example, you're considering creating a new logo. Use a bright yellow colour and a simple triangle shape to get attention and show ambition. The empathic approach is like the yellow colour, empowering people. The ego driven approach triangle symbolises a strong foundation for growth. Both statements are correct. They address different parts of decision-making and work well together. To create a solution, consider how these design elements improve it. Bold colours and simple shapes can connect people's emotions and capture their attention.

If you think this way, you care about your coworkers and want good things for everyone. Being resourceful and adaptable helps you grow and become valuable in your career. To be confident in your instincts, remember that creative thinking is essential. When trying to think to solve problems, ask yourself these critical questions. They can help you become more resourceful and adaptable, improving your problem-solving skills.

How can you calm your mind to access your thoughts and ideas while problem-solving?

How can you improve your creative thinking to find new solutions to challenges?

How can you get better at breaking down complicated problems into simpler parts?

How can you trust your instincts and intuition when considering unusual ideas?

How can you ensure that your colleagues consider your ideas?

How can you balance being creative and practical when finding solutions to problems?

How can you better handle unexpected career opportunities by being resourceful and adaptable?

Creating an Action Plan for Continued Growth

Create a flexible plan to progress as you continue your journey. Make sure your future goals can adapt to new ideas and changes. To help your project improve, stay adaptable.

To start your new journey:

- Do a self-assessment.

- Look at what you've achieved and imagine your future.

- Keep an open mind about what might happen because sometimes things work out in your favour.

- Reflect on your strengths and acknowledge your weaknesses (there's always room for improvement).

- Consider your evolving values and identify your passions. You can find areas you want to improve and grow by reflecting.

Setting clear intentions is essential; you must transform them into positive action!

Have a brainstorming session with people who have helped you before. Together, imagine inspiring and practical steps to reach your goals. Consider the resources, skills, or knowledge you'll need for your transformative journey. This exercise helps you improve yourself and align with your purpose.

To get more help, tell a mentor or trusted person about your plans and goals. Imagine the fantastic person you want to be, even though you're already incredible! What qualities, abilities, or achievements embody your ideal self? Once you've envisioned this new version of yourself, let it serve as a compass for your purpose. Commit to keep learning throughout your life. Take courses, attend workshops, read books, network, meditate, research, or read Oracle cards. You'll soar, provided they align with your growth ambitions!

Ensure you have everything you need to learn and grow, such as time, money, or materials. Remember, achieving success requires effort, but it is attainable if you embrace opportunities. Create an action plan to represent your objectives, whether in your mind, as a to-do list, or a vision board. These are the steps required to gain your achievements. They'll help you see your goals in a more significant way.

Create a solid system to track your progress. Use a spreadsheet, journal, or tracking app to record successes and challenges. If you follow this method, your plan will stay effective and adapt to your growth. Try different ways to track progress and find what motivates you to reach your goals.

To follow your plan, stay focused and committed, even when things get in the way. To avoid feeling overwhelmed, focus on your top goals and remain concentrated. Remember to keep acknowledging your achievements and celebrate your commitments throughout your journey. Staying focused will be challenging, especially when you doubt yourself. But these factors are essential.

Make self-care a priority by exercising, practising mindfulness, and managing stress daily. Nurturing a healthy body and mind is essential for sustaining personal development.

Thank yourself for working hard, and thank others for their help. It empowers you to lead a more fulfilling life guided by your intuitive and empathic wisdom.

Check your progress using these questions as a guide (or feel free to create your own). You can assess what's practical, what requires adaptation and what you can let go of! It's essential to be flexible and open to changes in your plan. You'll recognise when your goals or strategies need to change. It allows you to continue evolving and growing.

Answering the following questions can help you grasp your action plan and reach your goals. Before responding, take a moment to read, reflect upon, and understand the questions. There are no right or wrong answers - only what resonates with your inner truth.

Which goals do you aim to do as part of your growth journey?

What significance do these goals hold for you? What drives your motivation to chase after them?

Which strengths and skills do you have that can help you achieve these goals?

What weaknesses or challenges could hinder your progress? How do you plan to overcome them?

From which supportive networks can you access resources to empower your growth?

What skills or knowledge do you need to get to achieve your goals?

What actionable steps can you take to move closer to each of your goals?

What's the timeline for these goals? Do you need specific deadlines for each achievement?

How can you assess your advancement and achievements as you proceed?

What daily or weekly habits can you use to stay consistent?

How can you change your action plan if circumstances or new opportunities emerge?

Who can you seek guidance, mentorship, and feedback from to improve your journey?

How can you care for yourself and improve your health as you grow?

What thoughts and lessons should you write down? Will tracking progress help you make the necessary adjustments needed?

To clarify your goals, understand what success means to you. Self-reflection will also provide insights into your strengths, weaknesses, values, and passions. These can form the foundation to align your intentions with your decisions. Regular meditation can grant you access to new perspectives related to your choices. Combining your instincts with your feelings lets you decide what you want in your career. Now, you can create a SMART plan. It should be specific, measurable, achievable, relevant, and time-bound. This plan will guide your intentions.

- 'Specific' means having a clear and precise final goal without uncertainty.

- 'Measurable' involves tracking and evaluating your plan based on specific and tangible indicators. You can measure your progress using clear benchmarks and see how close you are to your goal. Measurability helps you see if your goal is doable and lets you make necessary changes.

- 'Achievable' (or attainable) means setting realistic and practical goals. They'll be reachable with the available resources, skills, time, and effort. It would be best if you avoided ambitious aims to keep motivation.

- Being 'relevant' means your intentions align with your values and fit your goals. It should help you reach your main goals without distracting you from them. Relevant purposes help keep focus on outcomes that matter to you.

- 'Time-Bound' means setting a specific deadline for achieving your intention. It can be a single date or a period. Adding a time-bound element creates a sense of urgency and accountability. Ensure you stay on track and get things done on time; staying focused and motivated is essential. It will help you plan well and use your resources.

You can apply your smart goals to visualisation techniques using a vision board. Express your intentions using positive images, quotes, and symbols. You are the steps towards your vision. Strengthen your belief in your abilities and the desired outcomes. Display this board in a prominent place to serve as a daily reminder of your intentions.

Manifesting success is a magical journey combining inner growth with practical action. By assessing your progress, you can determine what works and doesn't to make changes. At times, the Universe may present better opportunities than you had imagined. Being grateful for your achievements brings positivity into your personal and professional life. You do what you want, welcome new chances, and stay positive. Reflect on the following questions to aid you in defining the purposes you aim to turn into reality.

How can the SMART criteria help you create goals that align with your intentions?

What does success in your professional field mean to you?

How can you better understand your strengths, weaknesses, values, and passions?

How does empathy affect your intentions and your goals' impact on others?

How can you make a vision board to believe in yourself and your goals?

How does being grateful for what you've done help you stay optimistic about the future?

How can you stay open to unexpected changes? Can you adjust your plans to achieve your goals?

How can you assess if your efforts achieve success and find opportunities?

Understanding the Energy of Moon Phases

Understanding the Moon's phases involves tuning into your emotions. Observe how they react to the Moon's changing position as it revolves around the Earth. The Moon's alignment with the Sun and Earth influences these emotional shifts.

From Earth, we can see different parts of the Moon during nine main phases. It commences with the Black Moon, in which there is no visibility. The Moon goes through a series of different stages. The Moon has different phases:

- New Moon

- Waxing Crescent

- First Quarter

- Waxing Gibbous

- Full Moon

- Waning Gibbous

- Third Quarter

- Waning Crescent

The cycle returns to the New Moon and continues for 29.5 days each month. Understanding these phases has significant implications in our lives. It includes timekeeping, tide predictions, and cultural or religious significance in different societies.

Many believe the Moon's phases impact our emotions, but science must prove this. By narrowing down these stages, you can study how lunar cycles affect your emotions. This way, you can welcome them and free up time to pursue your goals. Begin by identifying the start dates for the following phases:

- New Moon: signifies a fresh start and a clean slate. It lets you lay the groundwork for your intentions and any new projects. It is a time for fostering optimism and hope as you set your preferences for what you want to manifest. It can prompt introspection, urging reflection on how desires impact emotions.

- First Quarter Moon: you face challenges and obstacles at the beginning of your plans. You may experience determination or resilience in making necessary changes. It is an opportunity to check your progress and adjust for you to stay on the right path. On an intuitive level, you gain valuable insights to refine your journey.

- A Full Moon intensifies both positive and negative emotions. It is an ideal time for rituals to release energy and let go of what no longer serves you. Additionally, it marks the moment to begin manifesting your intentions into reality. This phase offers more profound insights into your experiences. It fosters emotional closure and completion.

- Last Quarter Moon: provides a chance for rest and reflection. It enables you to assess your progress since the previous New Moon. Express gratitude for your achievements and release anything misaligned with your original intentions. To create space for growth, listen to your inner wisdom to gain future insights. You're preparing for new beginnings at the next New Moon.

Use candles that match your chakras and perform rituals to enhance your manifestations. You can use crystals and spells at different times to strengthen your intentions. Harnessing lunar energy for manifesting is a personal pursuit. Some people find it helpful to focus on their goals, while others may not understand it. Follow your instincts and assess the outcomes of your efforts about your goals. Over time, you will likely observe the success of your expressions. Manifestation is helpful for personal growth and focusing on future intentions.

We must consider how the Moon's energy affects our experiences and beliefs. Take a moment to reflect on the following questions. Understand how the Moon's phases relate to your emotions to achieve your goals.

How do the Moon's phases connect to your beliefs and intentions?

What are the specific goals or intentions you want to manifest during this lunar cycle?

How do you feel during each phase of the Moon, and how can you use this awareness to strengthen your desires?

How can you connect with utilising lunar energy for manifesting? Does it hold value as a tool for personal growth and your efforts to establish future intentions?

What practices do you follow to connect with Moon energy and follow your intuition? How can you assess the outcomes of your manifestations as time progresses?

How can you use Moon energy to achieve your goals and grow?

Harnessing the Power of Manifestation

The Moon's phases are a continual reminder to maintain a connection with your inner self. Setting intuitive intentions can guide your path of personal growth and self-reflection. Using the Moon's energy for manifestation follows Archangel Haniel's guidance. Archangel Haniel can help you heal and develop your intuition using the Moon's power. She represents the caring parts of the Divine Feminine. She wants to restore balance and harmony and let go of things that no longer help you. These can be negative emotions, outdated beliefs, or toxic relationships. Haniel can give you guidance to help you understand your life's purpose. Taking responsibility for your choices and decisions leads to positive transformation.

Many people think it will come true if they make a wish. Manifestation means taking action towards your goals and believing they are possible. It would be best if you stayed open to unexpected opportunities that come your way.

Stay focused on your dreams and always act to encourage creativity in setting goals. It would be best to release any limiting beliefs or doubts hindering your progress. Each obstacle carries a valuable lesson to help you overcome future challenges. Find and fix issues that may hinder progress, and value conquering obstacles.

To stay on track, write down your goals, affirmations and visualisations in a journal. This journal keeps you motivated and helps you think, especially when unsure. Follow your inner guidance and assess the results of your manifestations. You'll witness the fruits of your efforts. Also, reach out to friends, family, or mentors with similar goals. They can help and motivate you on your path.

Remember Archangel Haniel's guidance and the Moon's phases to understand. Pause for self-reflection and contemplation in your journey. Believe in the process, even if you still need to make progress. Good things are happening for you. Patience and determination will lead to rewarding benefits. Manifestation is not a guaranteed method for fulfilling every desire. You can achieve your dreams by planning and trusting your intuition to use the Moon's energy.

The following questions can aid your intuition in the manifestation process. Take your time to answer the questions and think about how they relate to you. Assess how they align with your intuitive and empathic practices.

How have you been connecting with the different Moon phases? Have you used their energy to fulfil your desires? Have you used their power to heal emotions?

Are you drawn to the notion of seeking intuitive guidance from Archangel Haniel? How does this alignment resonate with your beliefs or practices if you are?

Can you identify a particular Moon phase that holds special significance for you? If so, what makes it meaningful?

Have you ever faced challenges or beliefs that stopped you from achieving your goals? If yes, how did you work to overcome them?

Do you have a journal where you write down your goals and experiences? If not, would you start one?

Do you believe that manifestation is more than wishing and requires proactive steps?

How can you stay patient and committed to your goals when progress is slow or challenging?

Setting Intentions and Goals with the Moon's Energy

Using positive and encouraging words is crucial to turning your goals into reality. Instead of saying, "I don't want to feel stressed anymore," you can say, "I want to feel more peaceful and calm." This change helps you imagine what you want. You imagine all the small parts and feel the emotions of achieving these goals.

Believing in your powerful capabilities is paramount here. To achieve your desired life, think, but don't doubt yourself. You need to understand that the direction you plan to take may not match your growing self-value. There is no need for any concern with this. You can't solve your problems because you're still progressing towards your goals. Trust your intuitive decisions, which will always be in your best interests. Life is a continual work in progress toward more tremendous success.

The Moon affects your creativity, emotions, and intuition. You can use its energy to help you grow. To start changing your life, let go of things that don't help you anymore. This process enables you to develop. It's an efficient tool for self-counselling. Remember that the guidance offered here (or in any other source) is not absolute. The aim is to uncover any unexplored elements. Understanding the root causes of obstacles helps you overcome them and make progress. Embrace new opportunities and overcome emotional barriers; gaining understanding is crucial. Ask medical, law, or business experts to help with your goals.

Remember the lessons from your past experiences to stay focused on your goals. They hold many valuable insights for your present to use as a tool for personal development. You can achieve this through various practices, which include:

- Conscious contemplation: helping you to reflect on your thoughts and feelings.

- Mindful journaling: helping you to clear your mind, making space for fresh ideas.

- Cleansing Your Energy: try taking a salt bath or shower. It can help purify your aura and bring clarity.

- Guidance Meditations: offers intuitive understanding for inner peace.

- Angelic Reiki: rebalancing your physical, emotional, mental, and intuitive well-being to promote harmony.

- Guidance Readings: provides clarity about your current circumstances.

These tools help you stay focused and empowered, but you still have free will. As you set firm intentions, trust your intuition to guide you. When you admit the need for positive change, you can seize control and live your way. When you set intentions, you make clear, positive goals that align with the Moon's energy. Start by working on your emotions and self-confidence to make your life better. Then, you can deal with any problems. Your intentions may involve self-improvement, self-reflection, mindfulness, and embracing change with gratitude. As you strive for progress, consider what you've learned and trust your instincts to stay on track.

The following introduction can be your roadmap to successful manifestation. Please feel free to add more if you need to do so. Establish an intention to nurture inner peace, relieve stress, and elevate emotional wellness.

- Make it your goal to boost your confidence and believe in yourself to achieve your goals.

- To attract nurturing relationships, transform negative emotions and old beliefs into positive ones. Let go of harmful relationships.

- Make it your goal to prioritise self-care and your well-being. It can include thoughtful journaling, energy purifying, and enhanced intuitive meditation.

- Invite what you want and let go of what no longer helps you.

- Decide to be aware of obstacles that could slow you down, even if you don't know about them.

- Embrace the idea that life is a journey to success. Stay open to new chances for personal growth and change.

- To stay empowered, focus on being positive and having faith, even when progress is slow.

Incorporating Moon Rituals into Daily Life

Integrating Moon phase rituals into your daily routine fosters a deep emotional connection. Being consistent is essential. It helps you stay connected and make needed changes. Create a personalised plan to make your fire ceremony at the full moon stage meaningful.

Remember, words are like spells that shape your intentions for the fire ceremony. Handwritten manifestations are at the heart of channelling positive energy. They help you remove unwanted elements from your life to manifest your desires. Be specific in your intentions to see them take shape as intended.

To ensure a successful experience:

- Plan and prepare for your daily ritual or fire ceremony.

- Maintain a dedicated manifestation or moon journal. You can write down your feelings and intuitive thoughts during the Moon's phases.

- Start each phase by gazing at the Moon, tune into your feelings and insights, and record any shifts in energy.

To make your rituals better:

- Add things like incense with specific intentions. You can buy them in many holistic stores or online.

- Create anointing oils by mixing essential oils and herbal infusions.

- Use them for cleansing energy and tools.

- Ensure your intentions match your desires. You can include anything angelic, spiritual, or religious.

To make your moon rituals stronger, add herbs. They create a positive atmosphere. Before using these herbs, make sure to research their spiritual symbolism. These herbs are great for setting positive intentions and promoting positivity.

- Sage: use sage in rituals and ceremonies because it can cleanse and purify. Burn loose or bundled sage to create fragrant smoke called 'smudging.' This practice eliminates stagnant or negative energies from spaces, people, or objects.

- Rosemary: an aromatic herb with symbolic attributes. The pleasant smell removes negative energy, helps you concentrate, and clears your mind. This herb is versatile. You can use it in rituals and practices to protect, remember, and gain insight.

- Lavender: a gentle aroma that can calm anxiety and stress. People use it for aromatherapy and to sleep better.

- Mugwort: a remarkable herb that intensifies the vividness of dreams. Those interested in their subconscious mind appreciate its mysterious nature and inner wisdom.

- Chamomile: a calming herb that can reduce anxiety and improve emotional well-being. It can also be a soothing tea—a valuable ally in your inner peace and healing journey.

You can use these herbs in your Moon or daily rituals. Make smudge sticks or sachets with them. If you light the herbs on your fire, they will create a calming, fragrant smoke. You can use the smoke at your ceremony to cleanse yourself, your surroundings, and objects. It will help you connect more with the Moon's energy. You can also improve your connection with the Moon by putting herb sachets under your pillow.

Crystals can attract positive energy and raise your vibrational frequency. They can also offer intuitive protection during transitional phases. If you want to use them in a fire ceremony, don't put them in the fire because you'll want to use them again. Instead, place them around the fire or candle. Afterwards, purify their energy using Selenite or the Master Healing crystal, Clear Quartz.

Here are some popular crystals you can use in your daily rituals and fire ceremony.

- Black Tourmaline: a powerful crystal renowned for its protective qualities. It guards against external influences. It absorbs and transforms negative energy. It provides a strong sense of security for people who want to feel safe and calm.

- Tigers Eye: a beautiful stone promoting self-confidence and courage. During times of change or when you need a self-esteem boost, it helps you think and stay grounded.

- Citrine: a radiant crystal that exudes positivity to stimulate creativity. It increases self-confidence by inviting prosperity into your life.

- Green Aventurine: a supportive crystal to nurture emotional healing. This crystal's energy brings calmness, optimism, and well-being. It helps renew with ease and grace.

- Rose Quartz: promoting unconditional love and forgiveness for yourself and others. It fosters self-acceptance, compassion, and emotional healing.

- Turquoise: a lovely crystal to express your feelings and intentions. It encourages meaningful conversations.

- Sodalite: a powerful crystal supporting personal growth through self-discovery. A valuable ally in aligning with your authentic self to gain clarity in various aspects of life.

- Amethyst: a crystal that protects during spiritual activities, like meditation and intuition. It is also a good choice for bringing a sense of calmness and serenity.

The Moon's energy boosts the power of your fire ceremony. Forging a deep bond with your inner self paves the way for transformation and renewal. The beautiful atmosphere allows for deep thinking under the moonlit sky. As your letters and dreams turn into fire, you use the fire's power to make your intentions come true. During the ceremony, your energy connects to the Moon. This connection offers intuitive insights for healing and manifestation.

Choosing an appropriate container for burning your intentions is essential for potential reuse. Options include a fire pit, chiminea, BBQ, and metal plant pot or bowl. If none of these is available, a tealight can suffice. You can also opt for a coloured candle that meets your needs. The following colours can assist with your intentions:

- Black: a valuable colour in rituals. It banishes negativity, protects, and represents transformation. It absorbs negative energies and enhances psychic awareness. The symbol represents new beginnings and can turn negativity into positive energy. It stresses the importance of focusing on positive transformation and protection in manifestation.

- Red: intensifying emotions and desires, igniting passion in romance, creativity, and personal endeavours. It represents bravery, courage, self-confidence, and the ability to conquer challenges.

- Orange: used for creativity and innovation in your art or work. It encourages enthusiasm. It infuses energy and happiness into your efforts.

- Yellow: enhancing mental clarity. It proves beneficial for making decisions and complex problem-solving and decision making. It boosts concentration, goal-setting, and productivity. Facilitating clear communication and improving self-expression enables persuasive abilities in manifestation practices.

- Green: a colour that can attract money and good health. The connection to wealth and well-being exists. It helps environmental causes and sustainability events by connecting to growth and nature. It also promotes balance in life and relationships.

- Pink: a versatile colour in manifestation associated with matters of the heart. Excellent for bringing love and healing to relationships and self-care. It can also bring compassion. It promotes kindness, empathy, and harmony and helps in emotional healing and recovery.

- Blue: representing calmness, peace, truth, clarity, and spiritual development. It is ideal for those seeking tranquillity, honesty, and intuitive connection.

- White: a versatile colour used in manifestation practices. It represents purity and getting rid of negativity and impurities. Providing a new beginning and clarity shows clear thinking and guards against negativity.

- Gold: a prominent element in manifestation rituals for financial success. People use gold in visualisation techniques to help them focus on their money goals. Gold can also help increase their wealth. It symbolises prosperity, achievement, success, and spiritual enlightenment. Boost your confidence and belief by balancing your energy and achieving your goals.

In the past, I have done many fire ceremonies, especially during the Full Moon. Once, I planned an extensive ritual to let go of negativity in my life. I also engaged in some spell work as guided by the Universe. I've burned letters and objects that symbolised my desires at these events. I buried the ashes after the ceremony. My neighbours have grown accustomed to what I do.

Sitting by the warming, crackling fire, I captured intriguing images within the flames. Passersby should have inquired about whom or what I was burning. Instead, they complimented the aromatic scents wafting from the ceremony. I have reduced these fancy rituals as I run out of space to dig holes!

I help guide Melissa's Ego

A foolish thought crossed my mind while burying the red-hot ashes in the hole. Teasing my ego, I had the idea of embarking on a barefoot walk across them. Luci stepped in, leading me to resist that inquisitive and impulsive urge to burn my feet!

It's essential to exercise caution when working with fire or candles. Fire can become uncontrollable if not monitored. If you don't have a fire extinguisher with water, make sure you have water or sand close by to put out the fire. Indoors, maintain a safe and fire-resistant environment. Keep flammable objects like tablecloths and curtains out of the way. When outside, be careful of things that could trip you or catch fire, like fences and sheds. Once you've done these things, you can use the Moon's energy in a fire ceremony.

Introduction to Oracle Card Readings as a Tool for Self-Discovery

Tarot cards have fixed meanings due to their long history and tradition. I prefer Oracle cards as they allow room for intuitive thought. They can help you discover more about yourself, like talking to a wise friend.

These unique cards can help you rely on your gut and comprehend various aspects of your life. The process of using Oracle cards is intuitive yet straightforward. To start:

- Focus on the present moment

- Clear your mind of distractions

- Pose questions to seek guidance on love, career, personal growth, or life

Shuffling the cards is the next step. You can use different techniques to choose a card, like shuffling or fanning the cards. Trust your intuition when creating personal rituals. Infuse the deck with your energy. Due to tradition, what feels right for you may not be suitable for someone else. Stick with your decision.

The cards can help you see your thoughts, feelings, and questions. The readings are helpful and compassionate. They show you how to improve and heal while guiding you. Enjoy the process without overanalysing responses; it's about exploration, learning, and development. When you incorporate Oracle readings into your life, it becomes a valuable practice. This practice helps you make intuitive decisions with grace and confidence.

Exploring hidden parts of yourself and understanding life's impact can be life-changing. These readings help you understand history. They show patterns and influences on past decisions. They guide you toward a future filled with newfound clarity and purpose. Recording your gut feelings in a journal helps you trust your abilities. To get better at reading with intuition, be patient and focus on your progress and learning. Harnessing insights from intuitive readings and Oracle cards transforms your journey. It cultivates a growth mindset essential for personal transformation and healing. These tools help you connect with your intuition and the wisdom of the Universe. They intend to inspire you.

It would be best to be open and receptive to intuitive readings and Oracle cards. It helps you discover things about yourself and overcome regret by looking inside. This journey enables you to face challenges with a vital purpose and self-belief. You can find hidden messages using Oracle cards and make better choices. With these cards, you can improve your future by practising and letting go of the past. Begin reading the guidance booklet for inspiration. Then, look at the imagery. Reflect on everything that points out to you. Research the numbers, colours, symbols, etc. All hold clues to the answers you're looking for. Sit in your intuitive mindset and see what springs to mind. Write everything down so you allow time for reflection.

To tap into your intuition while reading, find a calm, focused space to clear your mind. Establish a comfortable environment with practices like meditation or deep breathing. Inducing relaxation and a quiet sense enhances receptivity to intuitive insights. Your intuition improves with consistent practice, becoming a habit. Before any intuitive reading, clarify your purpose and intentions, defining questions for guidance. When you set clear preferences, your intuition becomes more focused. When you have a better chance of understanding something, you often feel it as a strong intuition. Trust your first thoughts because overthinking can confuse your gut feelings. Let your intuition lead you to a deeper understanding.

Start your journey of self-discovery and trust in intuition with 11 Oracle readings. These readings offer valuable insights about different parts of your life. They create a safe space for growth and healing without judgment. These readings can provide a new outlook if you need help with love, work, or personal development. Enjoy this explorative learning and development journey. You can use Oracle readings to make intuitive decisions with confidence.

Keep track of your gut feelings by engaging and writing in a journal. It will help you become more confident in your abilities. Harness the transformative power of these Oracle cards to navigate challenges. You'll unveil hidden dimensions of your inner self and cultivate a growth-oriented future. These readings can help you reassess your history and find new clarity and purpose. Dedicate yourself to practising. You can unlock hidden messages and make informed choices, rising above past experiences.

When you trust your intuition and initial thoughts, it helps you stay calm and focused. It allows you to set clear intentions. Embrace guidance for a profound understanding of this empowering journey. Above all, enjoy the process!

Lucis' Sixth Sense Oracle Spread will enhance your intuition and empathy. It allows you to trust them more. Approach the reading with an open heart. Be ready to embrace the wisdom from the cards and your intuition. While practising, remember, feel free to draw more than one card if you need to elaborate on the answer. Ensure you jot down all the information that resonates with you to reference it later. It can help you see positive changes that may have occurred unnoticed.

You can use this spread to help you make complex decisions in life. It will guide you through challenges. For now, allow yourself to enjoy the experience.

What role does empathy play in your spiritual journey for intuitive growth?

What is currently stopping you from being more in touch with your feelings?

How can you enhance your empathy skills while safeguarding yourself from negative energy?

How can your past experiences or traumas affect your understanding of others' feelings? What can you do to handle them?

Do you need to be more aware of specific people or situations to develop your empathic intuition?

How can you strengthen your empathic intuition even further?

What is Luci trying to tell you through your empathic intuition right now?

The Self-Care Oracle Spread

Lucis' Self-Care Oracle Spread aims to make informed decisions about your well-being. Approach the reading with an open heart. Be ready to embrace the wisdom from the cards and your intuition. While practising, remember, feel free to draw more than one card if you need to elaborate on the answer. Ensure you jot down all the information that resonates with you to reference it later. It can help you see positive changes that may have occurred unnoticed.

You can use this spread to help you make complex decisions in life. It will guide you through challenges. For now, allow yourself to enjoy the experience.

In which areas of your life do you need to show greater resilience and inner strength?

What challenges or obstacles must you address to overcome to enhance stability?

What can you do to better nurture self-compassion in your daily life?

How has your previous experiences influenced your current resilience and self-compassion?

Can anything help you be more vital and kinder to yourself?

How does self-compassion change when you criticise or judge yourself? What can you do to address it?

How can you strike a balance between resilience and self-compassion in your life?

Lucis' Healing Mindset Oracle Spread helps overcome self-doubt and heal regrets. Approach the reading with an open heart. Be ready to embrace the wisdom from the cards and your intuition. While practising, remember, feel free to draw more than one card if you need to elaborate on the answer. Ensure you jot down all the information that resonates with you to reference it later. It can help you see positive changes that may have occurred unnoticed.

You can use this spread to help you make complex decisions in life. It will guide you through challenges. For now, allow yourself to enjoy the experience.

What are the underlying causes of your self-doubt?

How can you recognise and become more aware of self-doubt when it arises?

How can you release and heal the emotional baggage associated with regrets?

What lessons can you learn from past regrets and mistakes?

What aspects of your life enjoy a more open and growth-oriented perspective?

What positive opportunities can arise from acknowledging and addressing old regrets?

What practical steps can you take daily to develop a growth mindset?

Lucis' Unconditional Love Oracle Spread examines how love is essential in your life. Approach the reading with an open heart. Be ready to embrace the wisdom from the cards and your intuition. While practising, remember, feel free to draw more than one card if you need to elaborate on the answer. Ensure you jot down all the information that resonates with you to reference it later. It can help you see positive changes that may have occurred unnoticed.

You can use this spread to help you make complex decisions in life. It will guide you through challenges. For now, allow yourself to enjoy the experience.

How would you describe your current state of being with experiencing unconditional love?

How can you enhance your capacity to love others while caring for yourself?

How can you offer love without expecting others to reciprocate it?

How can you accept love from others without judgment or condition?

What challenges or obstacles may be blocking your ability to love?

How can you embrace unconditional love that transforms your relationships for the better?

How can you make your love and platonic relationships better and more unconditional?

The Empathic Communication Oracle Spread

Lucis' Empathic Communication Oracle Spread helps you understand conversations better. Approach the reading with an open heart. Be ready to embrace the wisdom from the cards and your intuition. While practising, remember, feel free to draw more than one card if you need to elaborate on the answer. Ensure you jot down all the information that resonates with you to reference it later. It can help you see positive changes that may have occurred unnoticed.

You can use this spread to help you make complex decisions in life. It will guide you through challenges. For now, allow yourself to enjoy the experience.

Have you ever had a conversation where someone showed genuine empathy and intuition? How did it impact the discussion and your feelings?

Think about a time you provided solutions when someone needed empathy. What happened, and what did you learn?

Remember a time when you adapted your communication to match someone's preferences. How did it enhance the interaction's quality?

Where do you struggle with empathy and intuition in conversations? How can you improve?

How can you show empathy and understanding in your interactions? How can you offer solutions, too?

How do you stay focused and engaged during difficult conversations, including emotional ones?

How can you handle disagreements and differing opinions while remaining understanding and wise?

The Trust Within & Beyond Oracle Spread

Lucis' Trust Within & Beyond Oracle Spread helps you in different areas of life. It gives you guidance and understanding. Approach the reading with an open heart. Be ready to embrace the wisdom from the cards and your intuition. While practising, remember, feel free to draw more than one card if you need to elaborate on the answer. Ensure you jot down all the information that resonates with you to reference it later. It can help you see positive changes that may have occurred unnoticed.

You can use this spread to help you make complex decisions in life. It will guide you through challenges. For now, allow yourself to enjoy the experience.

What qualities can you draw upon to strengthen your trust in yourself?

What outdated thoughts or beliefs should you release to enhance self-trust?

How can you better connect with your intuitive guidance to boost self-trust?

How can you develop trust in your relationships by gaining valuable insights?

How can setting healthy boundaries contribute to building trust in yourself and others?

How can you build more trust and connections with yourself and authority figures?

What guidance from the Luci is there to assist you in trusting your intuition?

Lucis' Past Life Oracle Spread is to reflect and find your life's purpose. Approach the reading with an open heart. Be ready to embrace the wisdom from the cards and your intuition. While practising, remember, feel free to draw more than one card if you need to elaborate on the answer. Ensure you jot down all the information that resonates with you to reference it later. It can help you see positive changes that may have occurred unnoticed.

You can use this spread to help you make complex decisions in life. It will guide you through challenges. For now, allow yourself to enjoy the experience.

How have your past life experiences shaped this life's journey?

What past life skills or talents can you incorporate into this present life?

What challenges or obstacles from past lives should you be aware of as you pursue this life's purpose?

What key messages or lessons from your past lives are relevant to your current life path?

How can you align your decisions and actions with your past life purpose?

What signs or synchronicities from your past lives guide your current life purpose?

How can you align your life's purpose with unconditional Divine love?

243

The Reveal Your Potential Oracle Spread

Lucis' Reveal Your Potential Oracle Spread helps you see what could happen in your life. Approach the reading with an open heart. Be ready to embrace the wisdom from the cards and your intuition. While practising, remember, feel free to draw more than one card if you need to elaborate on the answer. Ensure you jot down all the information that resonates with you to reference it later. It can help you see positive changes that may have occurred unnoticed.

You can use this spread to help you make complex decisions in life. It will guide you through challenges. For now, allow yourself to enjoy the experience.

How are your current personal beliefs and values influencing you at this moment in time?

What areas of your emotional awareness still need healing?

What practises can help you become self-aware that leads to greater self-discovery?

What makes it hard for you to gain confidence and overcome impostor syndrome?

What aspects of your purpose and goals need clarification for understanding?

What special skills and traits can help you discover and achieve your true purpose?

How can you unlock your potential self-awareness to help you move forward?

The Career Empowerment Oracle Spread

Lucis' Career Empowerment Oracle Spread helps you find a job that suits your goals. Approach the reading with an open heart. Be ready to embrace the wisdom from the cards and your intuition. While practising, remember, feel free to draw more than one card if you need to elaborate on the answer. Ensure you jot down all the information that resonates with you to reference it later. It can help you see positive changes that may have occurred unnoticed.

You can use this spread to help you make complex decisions in life. It will guide you through challenges. For now, allow yourself to enjoy the experience.

What aspects of your career need greater flexibility and adaptability?

How can you balance being resourceful and empathetic at work while problem-solving?

What strengths should you embrace for a purposeful career?

How can you nurture gratitude and attract positivity into your career?

What steps should you take next to attract new opportunities in your career?

What is the potential outcome for your chosen career?

How can Lucis' guidance help you grow and advance in your career?

The Roadmap for Success Oracle Spread

Lucis' Roadmap for Success Oracle Spread helps personal and professional development. Approach the reading with an open heart. Be ready to embrace the wisdom from the cards and your intuition. While practising, remember, feel free to draw more than one card if you need to elaborate on the answer. Ensure you jot down all the information that resonates with you to reference it later. It can help you see positive changes that may have occurred unnoticed.

You can use this spread to help you make complex decisions in life. It will guide you through challenges. For now, allow yourself to enjoy the experience.

Where are you right now on your path to success?

What should your next short-term goal be?

What should you embrace and let go of on your life journey?

What obstacles or challenges should you be aware of?

How can you overcome any fears or doubts?

What can help you stay motivated and inspired to achieve success?

What would the potential outcome be if you followed your roadmap?

Lucis' Moon Manifestation Oracle Spread helps you connect and manifest your desires. Approach the reading with an open heart. Be ready to embrace the wisdom from the cards and your intuition. While practising, remember, feel free to draw more than one card if you need to elaborate on the answer. Ensure you jot down all the information that resonates with you to reference it later. It can help you see positive changes that may have occurred unnoticed.

You can use this spread to help you make complex decisions in life. It will guide you through challenges. For now, allow yourself to enjoy the experience.

During the moon's phases, what are you focusing your manifesting on?

What actions or steps should you take to move closer to your manifestations?

What challenges might you face when reaching your goals, and how can you overcome them?

What should you release or let go of to make room for your manifestations?

What changes should you make to ensure your manifestation is successful?

What lessons or insights can you gain from your manifestation journey? How can you express gratitude for what you have received?

How must you finish your manifestation and make it a part of your life?

Right now is a celebration of your journey through this book. Take a moment to think about your experiences and celebrate your achievements. Recognise your progress and strength that have shaped you. This milestone shows that you can chase your dreams and find happiness in the future.

It's a graduation, meaning completing and recognising personal growth, not finishing it. If you followed the principles in this book, you've changed a lot from the start! I appreciate your efforts, commitment, and courage to reach this point. Recognise both your supporters and those who haven't encouraged you. Of course, remember your impact on others as you went through this process!

Take a moment to think about the important milestones you've achieved on this journey. Contemplate the challenges you've overcome and the invaluable wisdom you've acquired. Is there anything you should still reconsider? Take a moment to reflect. It will give you insights into further growth, progress, and opportunities.

Reflect on your transformative journey using intuition and empathy. In summary, it helps you connect with your inner self to understand better. When you trust your intuition, you can connect with your inner wisdom. It enables you to understand what is essential and be true to yourself. Empathy allows you to understand the experiences and emotions of others. It fosters stronger relationships and a sense of compatible togetherness. Reflecting on your journey is easier when you use intuition and empathy. They help you see different perspectives.

Seeking feedback from mentors or trusted individuals can benefit your growth. These questions help you understand yourself better and plan a more meaningful future. Their wisdom, including constructive criticism and compliments, clarifies your transformative journey. They are helping you appreciate your progress and future direction. To make better choices, use your knowledge to plan your future actions. It can help you keep growing and reach your goals with more focus and understanding.

Embrace these profound ideas to understand yourself better, grow, and continue your purpose. Navigate your future path with compassion and authenticity. You're becoming the person you aspire to be. You can share your transformative journey with people you haven't met. Your experiences and wisdom can inspire others to start growing. Your choices today can create a better future for you and those you meet.

To gain deeper insights into your personal growth, ask yourself these questions. The strategies required will assist you in pursuing your ambitions. Take the time to think about your thoughts. They can give you clarity and perspective on your life's journey and where it could go.

As you reflect on this book, have any essential moments or milestones shaped you?

How has this book impacted your life, and what differences have you noticed in yourself?

Did you face any specific challenges on your journey, and if you had, how did you navigate through them? What insights did you gain from those experiences?

How have the people around you changed your growth throughout your journey?

How have intuition and empathy influenced your transformative journey? Have you connected with yourself by understanding others' experiences?

Have you received guidance and feedback from other mentors or trusted individuals? If you have, how has their input influenced your personal growth and development?

What insights have you gained from self-reflection? How have these insights guided your future actions and decisions?

Would sharing your life-changing story inspire and motivate others to grow and change?

What impact do you hope to create for others due to your personal growth and transformation? How has this influenced your vision for the future?

Celebrating Personal Growth and Achievements

Remember to celebrate your progress and achievements as you work towards your goals. It stands as a clear recognition of your journey through a motivational act. It's a testament to your unwavering dedication through your darkest moments. Fulfil yourself and maintain a positive and forward-thinking mindset during the celebration. Value your hard work; it offers you endless opportunities to grow. Take the time to celebrate and honour your achievements. It inspires you to achieve more in your personal and professional life.

When you reach a big goal, you can treat yourself and find new and exciting opportunities. Once you finish a task, buy yourself to a special gift, indulge in your favourite food, or enjoy a relaxing day at a spa. You could even create your own spa experience at home. You can have a simple weekend trip and make special memories by discovering new places. Or, why not celebrate your accomplishments with a big party or get-together? Celebrate yourself, and give yourself a treat that reminds you of your value. Your past successes inspire you to set new goals for your growth journey.

For now, savour this extraordinary moment with a profound sense of achievement. Each moment in life is unique and precious. Appreciating the moment is essential, as it is fleeting and irreplaceable. Cherish it because it will never recur in the same way.

Hey, let's see that wonderful smile!

Now, go ahead. Have a little dance – you've earned it!

Graduation Ceremony and Honouring Your Progress

Congratulations!!   Bravo!!   Well done!!

We are proud of what you have accomplished. We toast your ongoing journey towards a happy and successful life. No matter the path you decide to follow.

Do organise some recognition for your graduation ceremony. Track it as a personalised event, honouring your personal and professional achievements. The informal ceremony recognises your commitment and achievements in self-improvement from this book.

Remember, there are many ways to celebrate this final ceremony. You can have a quiet and personal moment of reflection. A symbolic fire-burning ritual to release your written practices (if you wish to let go of them). It can even be an elaborate public celebration with the ones who've been there for you on your journey. No matter how you accept your achievements, take them and expect what lies ahead. You have earned it through this challenging journey.

Luci and I appreciate your hard work. While we can't be there with you in person, please know we have been close to you every step. We have always been there in spirit, guiding you and sending you healing when needed.

Sending so much love to you,

Melissa Grewar - The Spiritual Engineer & Luci. Xx

P.S. Never forget, 'In Us, We Trust'.

ACKNOWLEDGEMENTS:

I want to thank those who have helped shape my transformative journey. Your support, guidance, and wisdom have been instrumental in my growth. I am grateful for the support and advice from different people and what I learned during my journey. I appreciate the help of many people who have made this process better. I want to thank the people who made my life difficult. You taught me valuable lessons that helped me find my purpose.

A special thank you to my best friend Lisa for believing in who Luci moulded into the individual I am today. See, we're not as completely mad as you once thought!

I want to thank the diverse community of people who practice energy healing and self-care. These experts focus on people's happiness. My book contains information from people who have studied practices. They include Reiki, Chakra Healing, Crystal Healing, Meditation, and Aromatherapy. To learn about energy healing or aromatherapy, find reliable local sources for information. You can also search from the following:

International Practitioners of Holistic Medicine: https://www.iphm.co.uk

Thank you to those who promote a life centred around love. Your shared knowledge and ideas about love form the basis for Unconditional Love.

I want to thank everyone who represents trusting authorities. The insights gained from experience contribute to my understanding. I appreciate the many things I've learned about these important dynamics.

Thank you to everyone who has allowed me to learn a psychological perspective. You helped me understand relationships, how people interact, and emotions.

I thank those who have taught me to overcome imposter syndrome. These ideas come from personal experiences and resources in personal development.

I extend special acknowledgement for the following:
https://www.projectwizards.ne - George T. Doran began the concept of SMART Goals.

https://woopmylife.org - Psychology professor Gabriele Oettingen for developing\ the WOOP method.

https://cft.vanderbilt.edu - Grant Wiggins and Jay McTighe created Backward Design.

https://positivepsychology.com/ - Edwin A. Locke, founder of the Field of Goal-Setting Theory.

https://gordonsmithmedium.com - I want to thank Gordon Smith for his valuable contributions to spiritual practices. His ideas and lessons have helped me explore and understand mediumship. His work has inspired and enriched my journey through regular practice. I am thankful for the wisdom he has shared.

https://radleighvalentine.com – I appreciate Radleigh Valentine's helpful insights and contributions to understanding Archangel Haniel. His instructions have influenced what I now know about Archangels.

https://spiritwalkercrystals.learnworlds.com - I thank Spirit Walker Crystals for her wise lessons on spiritual practices. She guided me in discovering and exploring psychic mediumship, healing, and oracle abilities as well as other modalities. Thank you for your valuable contribution to my spiritual journey.

I want to thank the Fire Brigade for always keeping us safe by providing a valuable service. We can enjoy the power of fire rituals in a secure environment. Thank you for your courage and dedication to keeping our communities safe.

Thank you to all my fellow Musketeers! In no particular order for you're all amazing! Sarah, thank you for your networking support, friendship, and belief in my purpose. Fiona, thank you for helping me understand my roadmap to success. Emma, thank you for encouraging me to continue when I couldn't see a way forward. Mayira, for your gentle love and kindness during a difficult time. Bela, thank you for being you. Kay, for kicking me into a business perspective. I hated every moment of it, but I so appreciate it now! Donna, thank you for gifting me my name on your stage! Andrea, for listening. The gift of hearing is a blessing bestowed on you. Lesley, thank you for being such a powerhouse.

Jon, for brainstorming my future from a mindset into a realistic plan!

Mitali, thank you for your insightful information on how to get this book into print

Mary, thank you so much for your guidance on how to finally put this book on a virtual and physical shelf!

www.annenglish@co.uk - Ann for discovering your true creative path so you could share your amazing gifts for visual communication. You have helped me bring Luci into illustrative life and in doing so, helped so many others.

https://www.thedigitaldoctor.co.uk - Donna for your intermedia wisdom; I couldn't have got this far without your much needed assistance! Thank you for helping me bring this book from the intuitive world into what we assume is the real world.

In conclusion, I thank Luci, my spiritual guide. Thank you for your everlasting support, guidance, and love, even if I didn't appreciate it then. I do now. I thank the Universe for trusting in me to fulfil my purpose. Your help and advice have been valuable in all my past and this life.

In Us, We Trust...forever...

Milton Keynes UK
Ingram Content Group UK Ltd.
UKHW040416300324
440343UK00004B/207